LOVE
Beats

ALIGNING YOUR HEART'S RHYTHM WITH YOUR HEART'S DESIRES TO FIND **FOREVER LOVE**

LAURIE WINN

LOVE BEATS
Aligning Your Heart's Rhythm with Your Heart's Desires to Find Forever Love

Copyright © 2015 Laurie Winn

Published by:
Transformation Books
211 Pauline Drive #513
York, PA 17402
www.TransformationBooks.com

ISBN: 9780996827102
Library of Congress Control Number: 2015952001

Cover Design and Typesetting by: Ranilo Cabo
Editor: Allison Saia
Author Photo by: Senses at Play Photography

Printed in the United States of America

LOVE
Beats

ALIGNING YOUR HEART'S RHYTHM WITH
YOUR HEART'S DESIRES TO FIND **FOREVER LOVE**

Dedication

This book is dedicated to my mother Sarah, who encouraged me to never give up on my heart's desire. To my wonderful husband David who brings joy and safe love into my life.

And to all the hopeful singles who are still looking to find their forever love.

Acknowledgements

A special thanks to the "groovy gals" who helped me sort
out my love life; my forever dance partner Linda,
my full-throttle friend Peggy, my YaYa Sisters Dyann
and Rose, my soul sisters Nancy and Jenny
and the "Dancing Queens" Trudy, Sue, Cindy and Denise.

Thank you for your support especially when I was off
balanced in love and off balanced doing the "Stinky Stork!"

TABLE OF CONTENTS

INTRODUCTION

I have a philosophy about life; in your twenties you think you know what life is all about. In your thirties, it's not what you thought it would be. In your forties, you learn to deal with it and in your fifties, you learn to enjoy it.

I am enjoying the happily-ever lifestyle. I live on an island in the Florida Keys with my husband, enjoying the resort-like atmosphere. Today, I live in the high energy of peace, love and joy but this approach to living was not always like that for me. I had two burning questions: "WHY GOD WHY?" AND "WHEN GOD WHEN?"

After decades of dating, I began to wonder why when I had joy, there was no love and when I had love, there was no joy. I couldn't make sense of my "almost" moments of finding love.

It was on my fiftieth birthday, when I became surprised that time marched on without a Prince Charming in my life. The milestone of having a mid-life crisis turned into a mid-life catastrophe!

I was a never-been-married career woman that worked in a demanding industry with no time for relationships. I was flung into menopause and still hoping for love in my life.

For many women, such a reality would have shoved them over the edge of despair or settle to be a nominee for the "Old Maid Hall of Fame." But I still had the desire to be married and live the "Cinderella Dream," even though I was old enough to be Cinderella's grandmother! I took a positive approach and said to myself, "Delay is not denial."

Throughout my life I used my willingness "to hope for the best" as a pulse to revive my longing heart, even when it looked bleak. I tried other methods of bringing a man into my life by writing "a list." I made declarations to the Universe to bring "him" in, I prayed "him" in, I rewrote "my list," I Law of Attraction-ed "him" to me and called "him" forth like Lazarus from the tomb. The men that came into my life were usually the wrong ones. I exasperated everything I knew to find a man, only to discover myself still waiting for one.

With each passing decade, I continued to pick out men that were not good for me. I finally made a deal with God and the Universe to help clarify what I truly wanted when it came to love and to recognize the timing when "he" came into my life.

I uncovered a formula to "forever love" in a system I call "Love Beats."

My method transformed my old fantasies of what love looked like to break free of the negative patterns of love that I had been accustomed to.

A "love beat" is a period of time in my life that I awakened to the spiritual and energetic force of a love from some of the men. The emotional and spiritual turning points helped me eventually avoid certain pitfalls that started to repeat and it became a GPS to my happily-after life.

According to Webster's Dictionary, "Love" is defined as an *intense* affection for another or a thing.

♥ *Love Beat*

Love is an energy, which means it's a vibration that has a motivation attached to it, which can be pure or polluted. Steered by intent, love is your heart's energy in motion and also a state of being. Love energy produces fruit when it is in motion; the type of fruit it produces, depends on the seed that is planted, positive or negative. Love can be experienced in physical, soul (mind, will and emotions) and spirit levels. When love energy is operating in its full form, it will produce fruits of devotion, desire and passion. It can also produce pleasure or pain.

The word "beat" has many definitions: to strike, to hit repeatedly to cause pain, to overcome, defeat or surpass, to outmaneuver, to progress with difficulty, or exhaustion and in music, it's the audible, visual or mental markings of the metrical division of time in the music.

By putting those two words together, I discovered it was an accurate description of my love lessons as a hard-working single career woman. I was a woman who had strong affection to love's energies-emotional, physical and spiritual-only to have a man's love energy strike me down repeatedly (emotionally, physically and spiritually) and cause me pain until I was exhausted and felt defeated.

I was looking for the high energy of "forever love," but settling for the low energy of another. I desired forever love, but I didn't know how to recognize it.

"Forever love" is not only a love that lasts forever, it is so much more. Forever love is a complete trust in the power of unity between two souls and the joy to walk forward together in every area of life. It is culmination of acceptance, affection, and attention; it's appreciation and the art of allowing each other to be totally transparent. It is the brilliance of the soul connection that delights the universe; it is the oneness that can be shared by two souls that live in divine grace. It is what I also refer to as "the power of us." The "power of us" is expansive, abundant and most of all joyful. Forever love never gives up and has the courage to move forward when the world stops moving. This type of love in motion is a high vibrational power that provides a true level of happiness. In all its brilliance there is healing, transformation and freedom. Forever love is both safe and divine and most importantly it has no connection to time.

If Forever Love is the end result of what we strive for in relationships, then what are the other types of love energies that infiltrate our lives in relationships?

I can tell you that it starts out as "safe love." "Safe love" is the dream of a little girl; it is the joyful twirl of childlike exuberance. In the midst of her twirl, God smiles and the universe sees all possibilities. It is self-expression and creativity, it is a whirlwind of positive energy waiting to happen, calling on all the angels and guides to assist it into its destiny. Safe love is nurturing, encouraging and playful. It is filled with discovery, wonderment and growth. Safe love is not only safe to be whom you were created to be, but it also gives you the freedom to express yourself completely without judgment.

What happens when safe love isn't safe anymore? It becomes diluted with negative energy, perhaps a negative thought or an unhealthy name that you were called at a very young age. Something stops the joy filled energy of a child's safe love, something suddenly affects the way they view themselves and it begins to dilute their self-image, self-worth and self-confidence. The worst part of diluted love is it keeps us from loving ourselves.

"Diluted love" is full of compromise, listening to just enough to make you doubt yourself in negative ways. It infiltrates our thinking to accept that "love equals worry." The energy around that concept creates a place of justification and points the finger at everyone but you. It is the cloudy judgment of being with the wrong people and is always waiting for you to make wrong choices to judge and criticize you until you beat yourself up with shame and guilt. Diluted love keeps you in bondage to low energy emotions that feed your fears and keeps you from ever believing in yourself. Diluted love invites more pollution into your soul until a person spirals into dark love.

"Dark love" is the most dangerous love of all. It is seductive, controlling and spell binding. It has hidden agendas and toxic behavior. It is based on fear and driven to negative energies of shame, guilt and apathy. It creates in us a belief that love and fear are combined, which is what makes it dark. It takes us by the soul, rips out our hearts and squeezes the life out of us until we have no hope left inside of us. It kills, steals and destroys our spirits and leaves our souls restless and unfulfilled. We live in the darkness of mental and emotional distress and we are too frail to live a normal, happy life. It is life completely void of joy. It is full of misery living in delusion, deceit and despair. The only thing that can rescue a person from dark love is one who is illuminated with "Divine love."

"Divine love" is a pure spiritual love that transcends time. It is God's grace, the Universe's green lights with the angels, spirits and guides working behind the scenes to get things done and manifest your heart's desires. It is serendipity in action and it manifests all the virtues of the spirit of God; such as love, joy, peace, patience, kindness, goodness, faithfulness, gentleness and self-control. It is supernatural and having divine love renews the abundance of possibilities. It gives you wisdom to discern accurately the negative harmful energies that try to infiltrate your soul. When you have divine love, you have the ability to love yourself in a healthy way. You come to the realization that you are a co-creator of your future along with God. It is the place where you know love in its fullest form. Divine love blesses the union of souls to be sent out to help others.

During the love beat system in this book, you will notice the beats are few and far between in the beginning of the book, but as I learned and grew on my spiritual journey, the beats get more abundant and rich with insights until the last chapter consists of my rhythm of life in my present state of being.

It is my joy to share what I have learned with you, not just to share stories but reveal love energies that surround your soul when you enter into partnership. It is my hope that you will be transformed to release negative love patterns in your life and start your journey to forever love.

CHAPTER 1

Safe Love and Big Dreams

It finally makes sense to me now. I came to this world as a soul transformer called the "Joyinator." I am a spiritual teacher that assists people with transforming their lives through Divine love energy. I am a specialist in a joyful soul transformation.

I recognized at a very early age the mind, body, spirit / soul connection. I can discern the energy behind emotions, particularly in love.

I believe love is energy and that we are saturated in "love energy" when we are in the womb. Babies' love energy is magnified when they come into the world. I believe it's their birthright to give and feel love's energy in the fullest and purest form.

I was a perfectly Pisces mystical child, very curious, growing up in the land of EZ-bake ovens, Barbie dolls and Etch-a-Sketch. I was highly sensitive to the love energy of my parents, but I was also a typical little girl with the "Cinderella dream." (You know, the one where the handsome prince comes to sweep her off her feet, and they get married and live happily-ever-after.)

The house where I lived may have looked like a typical suburban home from the outside, but there was nothing typical about it on the inside; it was full of Latin music, lots of laughter and joyful love energy.

My dad, Frank, was the ringleader of our family circus. He was a remarkable man from a borough in New York City. He married my mom, Sarah, and moved to St. Louis, Missouri to work as a cameraman at a PBS television studio during the 1950's. He was also quite the entertainer who played Latin Percussion instruments in a Latin Jazz Band, in downtown St. Louis. (For those who don't know anything about Latin percussion, think back to the days of *I Love Lucy* and Ricky Ricardo playing "Baba Loo" on the conga drum.)

I can remember sneaking downstairs before his band rehearsals to take a peek at all the equipment. I observed an assortment of gourds, timbales, bongos, conga drums, Clave rhythm sticks and cowbells the Latin culture uses in their rhythm to activate joy and dancing. My father was bursting with Latin rhythm and was the original timekeeper who set my heartbeat timing.

My mother was the spiritual one. She was the one who taught us about church and about God. Through the years she imparted her Godly wisdom through scripture, prayer and faith. She wasn't preachy but would always say, "Preach the Gospel, use words when necessary." She helped us all navigate through the rough patches of life with laughter, wisdom and godly counsel.

Safe Love was the type of love energy my parents imparted to me. Safe love from them felt like total acceptance, total affection and attention. I was always allowed to express myself and was totally appreciated for it. Safe love from them gave me the fullness of confidence in my mind, emotions, spirit and body. As a child, I can remember safe love and joy were a natural state of my being.

As a family in the 1960's, we filled up on Latin music during the week and Catholic spirituality on Sundays. I loved to hear my dad play the conga drums when I was a little girl. I would twirl around in every room in the house.

The bass tones of his conga beats would float up through the house to our bedroom and vibrate the wooden floors under our feet. It resonated with my heart. I allowed the rhythm of the conga beat to sync up with my heartbeat. The sound made me feel blissful, free and full of laughter.

My brother Bobby and I would jump from bed to bed and spin around in silly dances until we laughed ourselves to sleep during the band rehearsals. As a child, it was always easy for us to recognize joy. Joy was simple and love was safe.

At five years old, I can remember being spiritually aware for the first time. My mother sat on the side of my bed and taught me how to pray. We would pray together every night and I felt a presence larger than my mind could comprehend.

It was a comforting warm energy that filled my soul with a warm and tender love.

She started, "Lord, bless my little Laurie." Then I would say random prayers like, "God bless my Barbie doll, mama and papa," with my hands folded neatly and my eyes tightly closed. I had a reverence for God even back as far as I can remember. My mother would kiss me good night and tuck me in tightly. I never had bad dreams or felt afraid when I went to bed. I felt pure safe love energy and the protection of the angels who were watching over me.

One evening we prayed as usual before my bed time. (There was a picture of Jesus hanging on the wall of my bedroom painted by my mother.) After we prayed, she tucked me in for the night, but before the lights went out I saw the lips move on the Jesus painting. "Mommy, the Jesus' lips moved!" I screamed.

"No honey, your eyes are tired and are playing tricks on you." She assured me, but I saw the lips move again.

"Please, take the picture down, Mommy." I begged until she took the picture off the wall and walked out of my room. At that age, I really didn't understand the significance of that first spiritual sighting, except it had me wondering about Jesus. I wondered if he could really talk to me and I wondered if I could really hear him.

♥ *Love Beat*

The incident was a preview of the supernatural events that I would encounter later in life, and how I was able to see images that were etched in my mind's eye for long periods of time. It was also a time when I was aware of my confidence as very happy child. I was living in a high-energy state, sensing my self- power for the first time.

I was in kindergarten when my teacher revealed to my parents that I had a photographic memory. Having a photographic memory was like having super powers as a kid. I could win board games easily and could always find my dad's keys, but when I grew older it became a double-edged sword. Not only would pleasant images stay in my mind for long periods of time, but if I saw something ugly or frightening, they would also stay in my mind's eye for days.

At eight years old, I was developing my self-image and learning about life with the other neighborhood kids. It was easy to attract fun and playful learning partners and I became very popular. At school I had a couple of instances with supernatural energies. I saw a blur of my guardian angel protect me from a woman who ran a stop sign. I remember I had a feeling of protection like I was in a bubble, safe from harm. As a little girl with little girl faith, I believed I was in the palm of the hand of God.

At age eight, one summer evening, my family was at-tending a backyard cookout at a neighbor's house. My brother and I were playing a game in the bedroom with the other kids called "Time Bomb" by Milton Bradley. I remembered seeing the black and white commercials with the announcer saying, "Time Bomb, What-a-game!"

The commercial was a happy group of kids in a circle, laughing and screaming with glee while passing around a toy bomb. When the bomb exploded, the kid holding it was out of the game. I remembered the advertisement so vividly and I playfully imitated the announcer's voice when we picked up the box to play.

Our game progressed until the only remaining players were my brother, a neighbor and myself. The bomb was ticking faster and faster and we were getting more excited. Caught up in the energy of excitement, my brother threw the bomb directly at my face. I could feel the sting of the hard plastic slap my face as the timer went off, I cringed with pain.

♥ Love Beat

The bomb timer going off was a symbol of what would follow me throughout my dating relationships. Simply put, Game Over! What I mean is my "game" which was my self-worth imploded and the course of my emotional development was diluted. I was stunted with an unworthiness energy that I carried inside of me the majority of my life.

"You're out!" Bobby said with glee and the other kids in the room started laughing with him. My lip was throbbing and when I looked down at my white shorts, I saw blood dripping from my face. I instantly put my hands across my mouth and ran into the living room where my mother was sitting with her friends. Tears exploded from my eyes as I told her what happened.

"Let's go in the bathroom and clean your lip," she said as she took me by the hand and led the way.

She took a clean wash towel and soaked it in cool water. "Let's see honey," she said as she gently wiped the blood off my lip. "Oh honey, your lip is split."

At that point I could feel my heart beating fast, but time stood still. I began to entertain thoughts about my looks (and looks were very important at eight years old). I could feel the emotion of fear rising up inside of me until I started trembling. I was afraid to look in the mirror, fearful as to what I would see.

My dad came running in the house from the backyard huffing and said, "What happened?" My mother calmly explained to him what had happened and I could see his expression of concern. He rushed into the bedroom where Bobby was holding the toy bomb.

"I didn't do anything." Bobby began to squeeze out his crocodile tears. "I didn't mean to…," he cried.

I could hear my dad ask, "What happened?" and everyone began speaking at once.

"One at a time," I heard him say calmly and I stayed in the bathroom with the washcloth pressed against my lips. Tears continued to stream from my eyes and rolled down my cheeks, and the constant pulsating of my lip had aroused my curiosity. I stood up on my tiptoes to investigate the damage in the mirror and as I did, I felt like I was in slow motion. I gradually opened my mouth and my front tooth had been broken and my top lip was swollen with dried blood.

I inspected my smile and immediately felt embarrassed; I instantly felt self-conscious of how I looked to others. My thoughts gravitated to looking hideous and unattractive.

"I'm ugly," I said to myself in the mirror.

My broken smile and explosive words did more damage than just my physical appearance. The time bomb destroyed my self-image. It shattered my self-confidence and ignited a negative energy force that rooted the concept of not loving myself.

I began to compare myself with other kids and hid my smile. The image in the mirror was embedded in my photographic memory and it created a distorted way of viewing myself. The self-defeating, diluted self-image built a foundation into my heart and I began to feel repulsive. The negative energies began to swirl around my mind and caused other negative emotions to attach to it.

The merging of negative emotions, thoughts and feelings resulted in low self-confidence and low self-esteem, but put a high focus on what was missing, my joy. Self-limiting beliefs like, "I'm not pretty enough," began to infiltrate my daily thinking and before I knew it, I had ushered in a spirit of rejection over my life.

My Cinderella dream slowly turned into a big girl reality of never going to prom, a homecoming or any high school dance. Living under the shadow of shame stunted my emotional growth. My timing was different than other girls my age who were happy attending all the school social activities. I became rebellious and judgmental, always feeling like the observer waiting for my turn to be picked.

After high school, most of my girlfriends had boyfriends or would talk about their strategies for getting noticed by the opposite sex. But I would never allow myself to think that way, I had grown into the gangly, frizzy-haired girl who was never picked for anything. I acquired the belief "I didn't deserve" a handsome prince to sweep me away.

I buried my low self-esteem with jokes and witty conversations. I morphed into the funny girl with the fun personality, but it was only masking the pain of rejection lurking around on the inside.

I discovered that if I laughed with people, the energy surrounding the laughter would temporarily bring me the joy I was lacking. I proved that theory, time and time again to help me cope with adolescence. I sought out a group of girlfriends who had similar things in common especially dancing. I refer to them as "Dancing Queens."

My group consisted of five handpicked girlfriends with a pact; no matter what we did or where we were, we would dance and have fun together. We were there for each other, like family. We kept each other safe on our outings across the bridge to Illinois, (where it was legal to drink at age 18). We made our "rounds" several nights a week to support our habit of dancing to live music. My life tempo seemed to pick up and I was looking at my circumstances with a bit more positive outlook. The collective cadence of my girlfriends kept me in a happy state of mind.

The collective energy of the group was laughter. In the group it was easy to express myself, be creative and fun creating silly dances, but during my time alone, I was still living in fear-based energy and becoming more mindful of each passing year of time.

For laughs I made up the "Stinky Stork." It was my signature dance where I stood in the middle of the dance floor on one leg snapping my fingers to the beat. I would begin to exaggerate the beat by moving different body parts and standing on one leg. The free leg popped up in the air and went in every direction it wanted to go. It was silly, ridiculous and contagious.

Sue was usually the one to point me out to the others, "Look! Laurie's doing the stinky stork!" My friends came from each corner of the dance floor to join me to perform our silly dance moves and laugh together.

I loved the way dancing made me feel. I felt blissful and free. I didn't feel any pain or rejection. I was approachable and fun loving. I would get glimpses of the same unbridled joy that I experienced as a little girl while I twirled to the beats of my dad's music. I would be enthralled in the rhythms and be in a trancelike state, allowing the music to transport me far away. My spirit was back in its natural state of joy for the moment.

During those moments, time stood still and magic began to happen. Men couldn't resist me as they watched my movements become enthralled in the music. Like a hypnotic potion, they were intoxicated by my musicality and were compelled to ask me to dance. Their acceptance made me feel worthy and validated. I lived in each moment of dance and was inebriated by the joyful carefree energy. I didn't need alcohol or drugs, just the rhythm of the music and the beat of a drum.

When the music stopped I would slowly go back to being a clumsy inexperienced young woman, haphazardly navigating through a sea of emotions. Most of my girlfriends spent a good deal of time pontificating about love and talking about guys. I had come to terms about my attractiveness and my new past time of dancing gave me confidence, also interest from the opposite sex.

One lazy Saturday afternoon, my girlfriend Trudy came over to pick me up to go shopping. We were sitting on my bed and I was telling her all about my second date with a new possibility named Randy. I was putting on my denim jacket when I heard the phone ring. I crossed my fingers up in the air and showed them to Trudy. I was secretly hoping it was Randy calling for a third date.

I heard my mother's voice from the kitchen, "Laur-rie, Randy is on the phone for you!"

I hopped off the bed, quickly shoved my feet in my clogs and scurried down the hall to talk to him. Randy was a hot catalog model for a department store. We had such a good time that I was hopeful for another date.

My feelings were naïve about men. I had limited experience dating, but lots of fantasies about Mr. Right. I was a victim of romance novels, magazine ads and television commercials, where beauty was everything and character was something you would only see in a movie.

I was hopeful for a relationship with Randy, but I needed to be cool about it. I put the phone up to my ear and smiled. "Hello?"

"Hey beautiful!" he said. "What are you up to?"

Before I plopped down on a kitchen chair, I leaned out into the hallway and gave Trudy a "thumbs up" sign.

"Nothing much, I'm hanging with Trudy trying to decide where to go tonight."

My mother was by the sink and turned around. I motioned her out of the room for some privacy and she walked downstairs to check on the laundry. My attention quickly came back to the conversation with Randy.

"Why don't you come up to Night Gallery and meet me there? I have something to show you."

I was curious, "What? What do you have to show me?"

"I bought a new car! I got a Triumph Spitfire and I want you to see it!"

I was flattered by the invitation. "That's cool! I would love to see it! Do I get a ride?"

"Of course you do," answered Randy. "That is why I called. I want you to be the first to ride in it! You will look so good in my car!"

I was lapping up his comments like a kid with a big bowl of ice cream. I didn't care if he meant them or not, I just couldn't get enough. I was confident I could convince Trudy to go to the nightclub.

"I will make sure we're there I can't wait to see you... and your new car!" I hung up the phone and skipped down the hall. Trudy could tell by my enthusiasm that I was super stoked and agreed to go.

My mind was racing; I had a hot new boyfriend with a hot new convertible sports car. I felt as if it was finally my time to have the fairy tale and I was on top of the world.

That evening the Dancing Queens piled into Trudy's car and between the loud music from the radio and the ride to our favorite place, Night Gallery, I told them about my two dates with Randy. They could tell I was impressed with him and how much I was looking forward to seeing him that night.

"Wow, so you really like this guy?" asked Denise

"Yeah, I think I do! He is good looking and we have things in common but I'm still trying to figure him out. I can't understand how a great looking guy like him could be interested in me."

Cindy turned down the music and said, "What do you mean, you are funny and cute. You really don't give yourself enough credit, Laur."

Denise chimed in, "Yeah what are you talking about? I know several guys that want to ask you out, but they are afraid to do it. You are always putting out a tough girl vibe."

"Really?" I looked puzzled. I didn't think I was the tough girl type, but apparently my intimidating outer appearance was a way of protection for the deep emotions still brewing on the inside of me.

"Who said they were interested in me?" I asked.

"Billy for one, he has asks about you every time you are in here. Do you know him?" she asked.

"Yeah, I know him, he is one of the best dancers in this place. He is interested in me?" I was shocked at the revelation, but distracted by a good song on the radio and started snapping my fingers to the beat.

"Oh, I love this song!" Cindy said from the front seat. The melody of "Slow Ride" came on the radio.

"Turn it up!" Denise screamed.

The voices of my friends' conversation turned into a joyful chorus of young women singing and having fun, "Slow ride, take it easy" We all sang in three-part harmony while Trudy kept her eyes on the road and her hands on the wheel.

♥ Love Beat

Having more spiritual maturity or having more self-worth would have given me more intuition to discern the chorus lyrics as a warning, but I kept on enjoying the ride across the bridge with my friends. I hadn't learned to listen to my intuition and I didn't know I could have heeded the caution to slow down my revved up emotions to a practical stranger. I was young and energetically living in a lower vibration of "longing" instead of a place of wholeness. I was still in the "to me" state of awareness and the "pick me" state of energy.

We arrived to a crowded parking lot where I searched for Randy's new car, but didn't see it. Pumped up people were already standing in a line to get in and we hopped out of the car to join them while Trudy looked for a place to park. I yelled, "We'll save you a seat if we find a table!" and the rest of us scurried to the end of the line.

I could feel the excitement building and said, "This place is crazy. It looks like it will be a good night!"

Denise replied, "Yeah, there is certainly something in the air. Is there a full moon?"

"It sure seems like it!" Cindy said as she pointed to some guys pushing each other in the parking lot.

After standing in line for twenty minutes we entered the bar and claimed a table as "home base." Everyone put their jackets and purses down and scattered in different directions. I was setting my purse on the table when a bartender friend approached me and said, "Laurie, Randy called to tell you he was going to be here later. He had to wait for his friend to get off work and they were coming together sometime about 11pm. OK?"

My excitement turned to disappointment and I said, "Yeah, OK, sure. "

I didn't dwell on the news for long as I heard the music starting which usually meant that the dancing queens were ready to come from every corner of the bar to hit the dance floor. Once we all were assembled on the dance floor, one song led to another and it turned into a dance marathon that kept us dancing throughout the first set.

We danced the "Stinky Stork" as our finale before the break. The energy of our dance was like no other; we had half the crowd on the floor dancing on one leg and continued to laugh about it as we walked to the table to catch our breath.

Trudy alerted me and pointed towards the front door, "I think I see Randy coming in the bar!"

We got to our table, still talking to each other when I turned to see Randy hustling through the front door looking all around. I caught his eye and waved him over to our table. He came over and pulled me close for a kiss. I felt like I was the only girl in the room and kissed him back.

"You look great, babe!" He was beaming and I felt like a million bucks, I was on cloud nine from all the attention after the dance.

"Hi! This is our table if you want to put your jacket on one of our chairs," I said with a smile.

"OK, in a minute. Let's get a round of drinks here, I only see water on the table."

Denise came up to the table winded and said, "Make mine a soda. I don't drink!"

He ordered a whisky and beer for himself and I had a wine spritzer. We began our conversation about his car. "Did you drive your new car here?"

"Oh yes, you should see it! I drove with the top down, even though it is a little chilly. I'll take you outside to see it in a minute." He was looking all around and the conversation was awkward.

"Are you looking for someone?" I asked.

"Well sort of. I came with a friend and was looking to see where he was."

I tried to ask him other questions, but he seemed preoccupied. For a moment I felt insecure and I wondered if his ex-girlfriend had entered the bar without me seeing her. I could feel my insecurities start to mount up, but he turned his attention towards me again. I couldn't understand why I was feeling so uncertain; I kept thinking he was so handsome other women were going to start hitting on him. The old familiar feelings of "not being good enough" began to seep into my moment. Until he interrupted my negative thoughts with his flattering words.

"You look great! I like what you have on." He was full of compliments and with each one, he charmed his way back into my "cloud nine" moment. I liked hearing the sound of him telling me I looked good, but for some reason I doubted he was sincere. I felt as if there was an undercurrent of dark energy that was deeper than his words. There was also an implied cockiness that I was picking up on from him. His conversation became judgmental, as he scanned the crowd, until it turned arrogant and self-righteous. His ego was inflated and he was brimming with more confidence than I had ever experienced in our two outings.

He began to share his story about the new car. "So, this is how I got the car. I was doing a modeling gig and the photo shoot was on location at a funky brick industrial park by the river."

"The photographer had the car as a prop and told me to pose in it. He told me that I was a natural fit. When the photo shoot was over, I walked around the car to check it out. I asked where he got it and the guy responded by asking me if I wanted to buy it I told him yes and we worked out a deal...and ta-da here I am!" He opened his arms as if he were embracing the world, but he was just showing off to say, "Look at me, I have arrived!"

As he rambled on about his newfound fortune, I noticed he wasn't the humble polite guy I went out with earlier in the week. Instead he was full of pride and thought he was some Hollywood movie star all because of a prop used in a photo shoot.

My intuition couldn't shake the feeling that he was just a jerk. In a matter of minutes I saw him change like Dr. Jekyll and Mr. Hyde. I became disenchanted and began my "pull-away-from-him" escape routine, but his continued flirtations enticed my curiosity to see the magical car that changed the personality of my Mister Perfect. Before I went to the parking lot, I honored the "Dance Queen Sista Pact." My ladies and I made a vow to alert one of the "queens" if we were doing anything outside our group alone.

I had combed the club looking for Trudy and finally found her under the stairs in a lip lock with a guy she had dated before. She came up for air long enough for me to tell her about going out to the parking lot to see Randy's new car. I also informed her I would be back inside when the band started playing again.

Thoughtfully she said, "I'll keep an eye on your purse and watch for you to come back in."

Feeling somewhat protected, I headed out to the parking lot with Randy. He slung his arm around my neck and leaned on me as we walked out the door. He was a big man and I could barely walk from the weight of him, but supported him as he walk towards his parking space.

During the short journey, it appeared to me that he had too many beers as his mood shifted from being overly affectionate to offensive. I didn't know how to decipher the mixed messages. My limited wisdom and lack of experience didn't discern the behavior of a man pumped up on his own accomplishments and the smell of a new car. I didn't know that too much of a good thing could make a normally humble person turn into a pretentious snob with a self-serving ego who slammed down whiskey.

I began to feel nervous energy and I should have been more in tune with the "fight or flight" feelings, instead I thought I was just being silly. My nerves disappeared when we approached the new convertible.

"Look at her! Isn't she a beauty?" He beamed with pride and took the end of his tee shirt and rubbed a smudge off the bumper. I had to give him the benefit of the doubt, no wonder he was so proud of getting this car. He deserved to be happy about it; it was a great looking car and he looked really good in it.

"YES! It's so cute!! Look at it! Can we sit in it?"

The excitement about the car dulled my previous warning senses. I gave him the benefit of the doubt and ignored my intuition.

"Yes! Check out this stereo! It rocks!" He turned on the radio and cranked up the music. It was a classic rock song from the rock group Bad Company and I completely forgot about his arrogance and began to enjoy the fun of the moment.

💜 *Love Beat*

"Bad Company" was another sign that was trying to get my attention that evening but I was too caught up in the moment to listen. "Good loving, gone bad" was the chorus of the song and the message the Universe was trying to send to me at the time. My judgment was cloudy and my will was weak. I just wanted to have fun and be accepted.

I felt the sound of the bass drum come through the stereo and instantly began "chair dancing" with breaks in between to play an "air guitar" solo and to sing the chorus out loud. Onlookers passed by us in the parking lot and complimented the car and our kick-ass stereo.

Both of us arrogantly snubbed them, said something critical and kept having our own fun, acting as if we didn't even notice the attention. In the moment, I felt privileged. I could describe it as an interesting combination of power and desire.

💜 *Love Beat*

I was actually feeling the powerful energy of his confidence. It was my first experience with this sort of elevated ego, because I was still living in the negative energy of low self-esteem ever since the "Time Bomb" exploded into my life. I had not experienced that level of self-worth in a person or in myself. It came across as cocky and arrogant, and I had no idea of the impact it would have on me.

He pulled out a bottle of Jack Daniels from under his front seat when the song was over. "Here have a swig!" He took a gulp and passed it to me.

"No thanks, I don't like that stuff. I just chugged the rest of my wine spritzer, I'm good."

He sighed in disgust and shoved the bottle closer to my face, "Just have a swig; we have to celebrate my new car!"

I didn't want to be a spoiler so I said, "OK," and took a small little sip. I pretended to take a big gulp and scrunched up my face with dislike of the taste. Not only did I hate the taste of the whisky, I detested how he forced me to have a drink and certainly didn't approve of the way he converted back to being so arrogant.

Another tidal wave of high alert hit me with all my senses aware of the red flags waving in front of my face. The fight-or-flight energy now coursed through my body. I was convinced to plan my escape when I heard the first chord of the band over the P.A.

I cleverly said, "Hey, the band is starting up. Let's go inside!"

At that moment the bass player plucked the strings of his guitar as a cue to get the other members up on the stage.

I said it again, "Let's go, they're starting! I want to go in!"

"OK, in a minute, I really didn't get to kiss you yet. Come with me, I have something else to show you but you have to follow me." He took me by the hand and led me down the path near the parking lot.

I didn't know what he had to show me and I was feeling insecure about it. I wanted to go back inside where I knew I would be safe, but he clutched my hand tighter. I pulled away in jest and he jerked my arm sternly to follow him. He took me to the far side of the building out of sight from the entrance and parking lot. He stood behind me and held me close to him with a firm grip around my waist. I felt more helpless, the tighter he gripped me and I shivered.

"Are you cold?" he asked. I nodded, but was silent.

"Look, I wanted to show you the moon. It's coming up over the fields. Isn't it beautiful?" He leaned over to kiss the back of my neck. I could feel an eerie chill down my spine and the hair on my arms raised up in fear.

"It's beautiful, but I am really cold. Can we go in now?" He seemed hurt by my lack of interest in his romance.

"No, not yet. Just stay out here for a few more minutes," he said with more authority and began to kiss my neck.

I was getting more nervous, when he positioned me toward him and began to kiss my mouth. I thought maybe I was being overly careful and kissed back reluctantly. He began kissing me more aggressively and I pushed him off me. I was overwhelmed by his behavior, but he lunged for my mouth again. I held out my arm against his chest, "Let's go in now!" I commanded.

I smoothed out my rumpled clothes and fixed my hair. I looked up at him to see his reaction and he looked at me with dark evil eyes, grabbed both my arms tightly around my triceps and kept me from moving.

I tried to pull away from him in terror and he pushed me to the ground. I felt the emotion of fear throughout my physical body and fear cloaked itself in my spirit. Randy intimidated me with his strength and size. I continued fighting him to let go of me and asked him one last time to let me go inside and he said, "NO!"

He was agitated by my pleas to go inside. He slammed me down to the ground again and held me by my throat so I couldn't get up. He pulled my pants down and began to fondle me. I managed to wriggle free, but he got on top of my body and straddled me. He tore my blouse open and buttons flew into the dark night. He lay on top of me, slobbering all over me, while holding me down. He told me if I screamed he would hit me. With his free hand he unzipped his pants and pulled out his penis.

"I know you want this." He was stroking himself and put his penis in my face.

I closed my eyes and tears rolled down my face. "No, I don't! Randy stop!" I cried.

"Oh no, I know you wanted this all night," he insisted.

He slobbered kisses on my mouth and his hot whiskey breath was smothering me. I was helpless with the weight of him and couldn't breathe. I tried to move and when I did, he thrust his penis inside of me, over and over. It felt like a knife cutting into me, ripping out my innocence and destroying my virginity. I remember just wanting it to be over. Each one of his thrusts were my pain and his pleasure.

After he was done, he rolled over and said something about it "being good" for him. He got up from the cold ground, zipped his pants and left me half naked in the cold. I was in toxic shock, poisoned by dark love.

I stayed on the ground, huddled in a fetal position for a couple of minutes. Freezing and traumatized, I managed to crawl up on my knees. The buttons torn from my blouse were scattered all over the ground and my pants were covered in mud and blood. I put my leather jacket on and zipped it up to cover my torn blouse. I stayed huddled on the side of the building, until I heard Trudy calling my name from the parking lot.

I came out from behind the building, wiped away my tears and clutched my arms around my waist as I approached her with a dazed look on my face.

Trudy asked, "Where have you been? I have been looking for you since the band started playing. Is everything OK? I saw Randy come inside, but didn't see you."

My expression was blank. I could barely walk. I was in such physical and emotional pain. I couldn't believe I was just raped. It was something that my parents warned me about, but I never thought it would happen to me. I was a good Catholic girl and thought I could use my judgment to save my virginity until I was ready to give myself to someone special.

Instead I was thrown around like a rag doll and discarded as trash. My fragile self-esteem was shattered by Randy's hidden agenda. Dark Love entered my life for the first time.

That night changed me. I lay in my bed, feeling very different about life and love. I didn't understand why I was assaulted and violated by someone I trusted. In one violent act of stealing my virginity, he stole my joy, placed fear in my heart and tainted my trust in men. I was polluted by his dark love and it changed the very core of my being, I hardened my heart to the possibility of love or of anything that resembled it.

💜 Love Beat

I didn't share my experience with anyone. The trauma of the rape energetically merged love and fear. It created one powerful cocktail of dark love. Fear settled into the base of my energy systems closing off my heart's ability to love. The trauma also began to fragment pieces of myself and plant a seed belief that love was fear. I was programmed to think that you can't trust men and men will hurt me.

CHAPTER 2

Diluted Love and the Dark Cloud

The days that followed, made me reclusive and I steered away from everyone. I internalized the whole incident and relived the emotional pain from the rape on a daily basis. I couldn't help thinking it was my fault; was I too trusting or too hopeful? My mind kept spinning around the why's of what happened. I felt ashamed for not recognizing such a self-serving jerk. I was devoured by the dark energies of regret, shame and condemnation until they took residence in my life.

Guilt consumed me. If only I listened to my intuition instead of listening to his flattery. I felt helpless.

♥ *Love Beat*

The dark energies that began as the thoughts "I'm not good enough" and" I'm not pretty" had opened the door

*for other negative energy to feed on. Thoughts such as "I
don't deserve love" and "I am broken" began to flood my
thinking. I initiated a life of a downward spiral with low
energies of shame and guilt. I felt as if something was
wrong with me, like I was a victim.*

In reality, I was a victim. I harbored the emotional pain for
weeks and I became a prisoner of my broken heart, shackled
to my shattered emotions.

My inner turmoil blinded me from other happenings in
my life, including family activities. I felt the joy in my heart
completely depart. I slowly morphed into a bitter young
woman, cloaked in a spirit of heaviness.

My friends wondered why I disappeared and were
concerned, but I didn't give them any clues of what happened.
I couldn't see them, because it was a reminder of the pain I
endured from our innocent outing.

My mother noticed me moping around the house and
invited me to go to new church. I recognized that she was
finding herself in a new religion. She had been listening to
my brother Bob, who was into the Born-Again movement.
He began sharing his experiences with God to my mother;
she was intrigued by his new behavior and fervent love for
God. I just wanted to think about something else besides what
happened, so I accepted her invitation.

I remember going to the large church with almost a
thousand people. There was a full band playing live folky
music. The lead vocalist had long hair, sandals and blue jeans.

He played worship music on his guitar and I really liked the sound of it. I had never seen this type of celebration in a church before and certainly not in a Catholic church in the 1970's. I began to look around at all the smiling faces and was interested in knowing what was so wonderful. Even though the music was gentle and beautiful during the service, I was still hard-hearted.

The ushers were friendly, kind and joyful as we walked through the door of the weekday service. It wasn't at all like the Catholic services I had gone to in the past.

I noticed no religious statues or monuments displayed, no pews to kneel on, no candles to light or confessionals to admit your faults. It was an open room with padded chairs arranged in a half circle pointing at the stage. Along the walls were silk flags of different countries and carefree people dancing in the aisles with scarves and tambourines. I thought I was in the middle of the hippie movement ten years too late.

When the preacher came out and preached the word out of the Bible, it was like listening to God speak to me directly. I didn't realize it, but my spirit was hungry for some kind of encouragement. I devoured the words of the Bible, like it was my last meal on earth. I began to feel my spirit and soul come alive again. I had hope.

On the ride home, I had a long conversation with my mom about God. I was confused by her sudden departure from her Catholic faith and asked her about her new belief system. She told me she was always fearful growing up and didn't understand the ways of God and especially the

Catholic religion. She said that she prayed alone one night in her room and God showed her scriptures in the Bible that made Himself real to her. Ever since then, she was learning things about God through the guidance of His Holy Spirit. She called it being Born-Again.

It all sounded too good to be true, but I was still too ashamed to ask anyone for help at that time. My soul knew deep inside, if I continued to feed it scriptures once in a while, the positive energy of the words would eventually help me feel better about myself and maybe in time I could know God like my mom did.

As the weeks went on, I started out slow by reading a daily devotional my mother gave me. Each day after I read my scripture, my mom and I would have long discussions about it. After my dad left for work, she started to watch a television evangelist and invited me in her room to watch one of the shows with her.

He spoke about heavenly encounters and angelic activity for believers. After the show was over, we lie in the bed staring at the ceiling, just thinking and talking about what it would be like to see an angel. My mom began to pray. First it was with normal words and then she made sounds I never heard her do before. She called it "her prayer language." She said it was the Holy Spirit talking through her and only God knew what she was saying.

I felt the atmosphere in the room become very peaceful and my body tingled. I opened my eyes and what I saw was incredible. The ceiling of the room had opened into a night sky full of stars, nebulas and constellations, (and it was still the middle of the day).

Our eyes were able to see angels as streaks of light, busily working for people on earth. Sometimes they would just stop, like they were waiting for something. It brought back to remembrance of seeing my guardian angel when I was a little girl.

We would say to each other, "Did you see that?" My mom would describe exactly what I was seeing.

Then she said, "Did you see that?" I would share with her exactly what I saw describing her images perfectly.

"We are getting a glimpse of the supernatural," she explained and when she said that, I saw an image of light at the foot of the bed. We held our hands together and said, "Jesus!" We automatically knew it was a holy presence and a divine visitation. The image reached out to us and we felt a warm sensation come over us. I strained to see more, but the illumination of the being made it difficult to do anything but bask in the tangible peaceful presence. I could slowly see the image fading as another energy entered our room. I saw a few jellyfish-looking beings trying to float toward the heavenly being. My mom said, "Do you see the bubble-headed boobies?"

"Yes, what are they? I don't like them," I replied. I wasn't afraid, but it made me feel uncomfortable and took away the peaceful feeling.

"I don't either." She broke our handhold and command-ed, "I rebuke you now and you have to leave this room in Jesus' name!" Her authority surprised me and the bubble-headed images disappeared immediately. The presence of the divine being got stronger and the light filled the room. I can't remember what happened next, because I passed out by the powerful energy of it. My mother told me later about a vision she had while I was asleep. She was basking in the presence of the Divine. She told me that she was "called" to be a prayer warrior.

After that spiritual encounter, I began to question my faith and whom I was as a person. I still had so many questions about love and life. I was confused. I had scars on top of my emotional wounds that kept me numb, but I still wanted to find love.

Instead I found myself living in the land of Diluted Love. It is a negative state of mind that I was subjected to when Randy raped me. Randy's negative intent, coupled by the violent act and my reaction to it, buried deep in my core. I was poisoned with fear and the safe love I once knew was diluted. I looked at myself with a weakened self-worth and the diluted love kept me from loving myself.

♥ Love Beat

The love that I once knew as safe was entangled with fear. It brought confusion to my heart and soul and it kept me intoxicated with a diluted love energy cocktail. A recipe of being addicted to the adrenalin rush of finding a guy, thought I was in love with him and worried that

I couldn't trust him. Fear energy made me believe that love equaled worry. I began to be insecure about any relationship and I worried whether he loved me or not.

Diluted love is full of compromise and justification. It whispers negative doubts in your ears until you start believing in them. You are not strong enough energetically to fight them off and begin to surrender to negative actions.

I was still living as a victim and felt powerless. The whimper of my soul was that I thought negative things about myself. I felt like they were true and everything bad happened to me. I craved to have love in my life, but I knew I didn't deserve it. When things went wrong in my life, I justified my actions and pointed my finger of accusation to everyone but me. I anticipated bad things happening to me on a regular basis. The negative mindset made cloudy judgment for picking men in my life. I could never get the very thing that I desired the most, a husband.

I continued to find myself in the wrong relationships and I couldn't trust men. When I began a relationship with a prospective guy, I would enter it with a false sense of safety. Before I knew it, the relationship quickly turn diluted by my distorted thoughts of what happily-ever-after should look like and their dark love behavior. It was a dance of power verses struggle and I became more confused.

A year after my rape, I moved out of my parents' house to discover myself as an adult and to try to be empowered. That is when I met John. I didn't like him at first. I thought he was the typical mind game player that had many women on a string.

John was the opposite of that presumption. He was a funny, down-to-earth guy who was very popular. He fit the mold of what I was normally attracted to. He was the typical tall, dark and handsome man, but I was really attracted to his ability to make me laugh.

He had a good heart, but after dating him for a few months I discovered he had a demon of his own to battle. It was an attachment to his ex-girlfriend of the past seven years, which I call a soul-tie. She used her "damsel in distress" charms often as a form of manipulation and out of obligation he would run to her rescue. Watching him run to her time after time got to be frustrating, but I was always willing to give him the benefit of the doubt.

♥ Love Beat

I learned that obligation or "having to" has a different energy level attached to it than "choosing to" energy. My desire was to be "chosen" and not have the obligation energy of "having to" be loved. I was still living in the adolescent energy of the "pick me" state of awareness, filled with insecurity.

However, being with a man like John helped me get past the sexual abuse I suffered with Randy. I was falling for him and wanted things to work out. When I was with John I didn't feel like damaged goods and made up my mind that our "love" would carry us through any of the bad times. It wasn't the "forever love" I was hoping for, it was love of a different kind, it was diluted love.

We had been dating for over six months and we intended to spend a day off together. John was going to call me to make more detailed plans, but he didn't call at his usual times. While I was waiting, I took the opportunity to run errands, but by the middle of the afternoon I wondered why I hadn't heard from him.

A thought popped into my head. It was a powerful intuition kind of thought that I call an "inkling" which told me to go by his house. This was out of my sort of behavior, I never thought it polite to "pop in" or sit outside a house to "keep tabs" but in this case, the urge was very strong inside of me. I listened to my intuition and drove by his house.

His car was in the driveway and another car was parked on the street. I walked out of my car and could see his door was open with only the screen door closed. I knocked on the screen door and no one answered. I knocked again and opened the screen door.

"Hello? John are you there?" I could see the light of the television on in his bedroom and I heard voices. I didn't know if it was from the television or if there was someone else with him. I slowly walked up the steps and noticed feet at the end of the bed.

I asked, "John are you sleeping?"

He hopped out of bed, zipping up his pants and when he got up I saw another pair of feet.

He said, "Baby, what are you doing here?"

I peeked in the room. It was his ex-girlfriend and my jaw dropped to the floor along with my heart.

My quick wit of sarcasm lashed out to mask the emotional pain. "I came here to see you, but it looks like you're too busy helping yourself to your ex!"

I ran down the stairs and slammed the screen door behind me. He ran down the stairs after me and said, 'Wait, I can explain!"

I didn't want to hear his idle words. I briskly walked to my car, hopped in it and drove off. The tears popped out of my eyes like a flood, as I rolled down the driveway and then anger built up inside of me.

"That's the last man who is going to hurt me!" I declared.

♥ *Love Beat*

How many times have we made a vow that we meant at the time of an emotional wound or trauma? It is the energy of that intent that stays inside of us. It can bury deep inside of us for our whole lives and do physical damage along with the deep emotional scar it can leave behind.

The attachment to the cord of a vow can actually leave us powerless, keeping us from the very thing we desire. The betrayal confirmed my belief of "men cannot be trusted."

Deep down inside, my heart was waiting for this to happen. I just didn't believe in love. I drove straight to my mother's house and told her what had happened. She gave me a hug and started to console me. I was broken and felt ashamed that I had another bad experience with a guy I trusted. My feelings were numb and I was catatonic, while my mother started talking about Jesus taking my pain away.

I listened half-heartedly and she asked, "Can I pray with you?"

I just wanted to feel better so I agreed to let her pray with me. As she prayed, it felt like warm rain washed over me. The prayer energy was so strong coming from her lips that I felt a strong wave of emotion come over me and began to cry.

She asked, "Do you want to ask Jesus in your heart now, Laurie?"

"I guess so." I was a reluctant participant, but felt safe enough in her living room to ask for help for my shattered heart.

"Repeat after me," she said. "I believe in Jesus Christ and the Holy Spirit. Come inside of me now and live in me. I repent of my sins and ask for your Divine Grace wash me clean of all my sins. I thank you Lord for saving me."

I said the prayer just like she said it. I stopped crying and felt my hard heart soften just a bit. I was appreciative for having such a spiritual mother and for teaching me the ways of God, but it didn't release the pain I still felt. She left the room and came in with a box of tissues and said, "God is going to be showing you things from this point on, only if you put your trust in Him and not in a man. You will be alright honey. You will see." She went into my old bedroom that she had made into an office and picked out a booklet to explain what had just happened spiritually. I read I was just born-again.

The ride home was interesting. I felt as if I was floating on a cloud outside of my body. I was physically exhausted with my rollercoaster emotions and when I got to my apartment my roommate Sue said, "John has called here at least five times asking about you. Where were you?"

"I was at my mom's and if that asshole calls here again, tell him I am not home."

I continued to tell her about my afternoon and what I had witnessed. Sue was my confidante. We clumsily muddled through life and love together, until she met her boyfriend Kevin, and later married him.

It was during a weekend pool party at our apartment complex where Sue and I met another friend who lived in the same complex. Her name was Linda and would later become my best friend. I was dancing with one of my neighbors to some funky tunes the DJ was playing when Linda came up to me and asked, "Hey, can I dance with you guys?"

I replied, "Yeah, sure. This is a great party! Do you live here?"

"Yes, I live over there," she said pointing to a neighboring building. We danced, talked and hung out the rest of the time.

Linda became my dance partner in life. We had an instant soul sister connection of love. During our conversations, we would laugh, cry and connect in a way that was different than all of my other girlfriends. We could be totally transparent with each other and were kindred spirits, especially when it came to dancing. We would later share an apartment together and traveled on countless road trips. I may not have put my trust in men, but I trusted Linda. I welcomed safe love again for the first time in many years. There were no hidden agendas, no schemes or manipulations. We were vulnerable with each other and living in authenticity.

I think the reason we bonded so well together was because we met while we were on our own in our early twenties, during a time when men were the most confusing. Through the years, between college, career aspirations and boy crushes we spent most of our adult life trying to decipher the mixed signals, bad dates or potential loves. We would spend hours trying to decode the man's behavior but could never come up with any concrete answers. When we didn't find the answers we were looking for, we would laugh about it and go out dancing. It was like the blind leading the blind, without any real guidance. I continued to settle for diluted love in my own life.

It also during that time that John convinced me to give him another chance and I ended up being attached to a six-year relationship with a man with so much control over me that I nicknamed him the "Thumb." When I finally had the courage to leave I just wanted to give him the "finger!"

I was so desperate to be loved that I tolerated six years of his lying, cheating and betrayal. I was addicted to the feeling of having love in my life and settled for his diluted love. The diluted love energy over the years displayed itself as being treated poorly, having no respect for each other and being taken for granted.

Settling for diluted love, made me feel lonely and resentful. I lost sight of myself and was extremely discontented. His love energy type was not satisfying. It was full of mixed messages and broken promises. I got to the point where it wasn't enough just to have a boyfriend. I longed for a different breed of love energy, one that I could build a lasting foundation upon. Instead I found myself with a survivor mentality, trying to survive his mind games. I was always trying to outwit, outplay and outlast the relationship before he evicted me from couple's "so-called" paradise.

I couldn't understand how my relationships started out safe, but over a period of time would change to diluted ones. I had a negative pattern of being addicted to the chase of a bad relationship and the pain of ending it. There was truly a dark cloud hanging over my love life and I couldn't find my rhythm in love.

After ending the yo-yo relationship with the "Thumb," I was brave enough to move to Florida to find my true heart's desire. I felt like my soul always lived in Florida, ever since my father took me to Daytona Beach at the age of ten.

I remembered when my father drove us on the beach during our family vacation in 1966. It was during the evening and I could only hear the roar of the ocean. I was so excited to wake up my brother Bobby who was fast asleep in the back seat and watch his eyes light up with excitement. We begged my dad to stop the car so we could take a closer look.

For me, it was love at first sight. I loved the way the water ran between my toes in the sand. I felt the ocean spray on my face and the rhythmic pounding of the water hitting the shore made me very happy. The powerful energy of the waves pulsated through me.

My life in Florida became a time of renewal for me. I was approaching thirty and still had high hopes of a family and a career. I put St. Louis behind me and embraced my new environment enthusiastically. I was hopeful and happy. I didn't have any ill feelings towards John, and felt for the first time that my life was on the upswing.

I began meeting influential people around town who challenged my thinking. One of them was the manager of the Judd's, (the mother/daughter country singing duo). We met at a bar and began a conversation. During our discussion he asked me what I would like to do with my life. It was like saying, "What do you want to be when you grow up?"

I looked at him and said, "I'm not really sure, but I do know that I like the broadcast television industry."

I really couldn't think of anything else to say, because I didn't really know what I wanted. I said the first thing that came into my mind. I was used to being around television studios and production trucks during my father's career. After my father worked at the PBS studio, he became one of the top-rated sports cameramen in the country. He was elevated to the "go to" cameraman at the high home camera position for the St. Louis Cardinals baseball team. He would take me to baseball games and I watched from the press box and listened to the announcer describe the games. I remembered it being cool and feeling excited every time I was at a game.

After remembering all the good times of television production, I pulled myself back into our conversation.

I think he noticed that I was thinking about the possibilities and looked at me right in the eyes and said, "You really need to look into doing that for a career."

I sensed the authoritative energy of in his words and it was as if he spoke seeds of greatness into my heart. With the focus on his advice that evening, I began to look at ways I could break into the television industry.

Through hard work and sheer determination, I put myself through broadcast production school and learned the ins and outs of television. I was hired as a sports video editor and quickly was promoted to the newsroom at WTSP-Channel 10. I guess it was in my blood.

It was a demanding and deadline-oriented profession, but I found the fast pace intoxicating and it became my rhythm of life. It was also the place where I repaired the pain with my father of leaving St. Louis. He wasn't happy with me living so far away, but I convinced him it was the best thing for me and working in the same industry gave us many things to talk about. I would call him each week and we would have long conversations about the business and he would give advice and share stories. I experienced his approval and it brought us closer, even though I was geographically so far away. He mentioned how proud he was of me for following his footsteps, which I was grateful.

A year after working in the industry, I felt I was in control of my own happiness once again. I was the most content when I was producing television shows and being near the beach. I found a satisfying career, but as the years rolled by I was still longing for the forever love of man.

♥ Love Beat

I started becoming more aware of time and my biological clock. I felt time slowly slipping away and aging began to seep into my subconscious. Society and media made it difficult to see myself in a healthy way. I was in an industry were one's looks were a commodity and I began to compare myself with younger women.

When I looked in the mirror, I noticed crow's feet and worry lines. I went back to my old negative patterns of not feeling attractive enough for a man to sweep me away. New negative patterns of trying to look younger than my age were always in the forefront of my mind. Again I tried to ignore those feelings by humor, making friends and burying myself in work.

My life was about to take a turn when I was on an assignment during a trip to Charleston. I was hired by the St. Petersburg Fire Department and was selected to video the aftermath of Hurricane Hugo. I was a part of the Pinellas County committee of officials to investigate the damage and to record video of what how they handled the evacuations. It was there I met "Anchor Boy."

"Anchor Boy" was a news reporter/part–time news anchor, he had the assignment to report on our group. I didn't know him before and when he introduced himself to me, I felt a spark.

While I was there working, I was caught up in the documentation of capturing the devastation and hearing the stories of the people who lived in the area. I felt compassion and sympathy for the survivors of such a devastating catastrophe.

After a long day of gathering stories, information and video footage the group came together at the hurricane headquarters. There were many people who came in to volunteer their time and resources, including celebrities. I watched people band together for a community and was deeply touched by the experience. I noticed Anchor Boy in the mix getting sound bites from celebrities and elected officials. When he finished his interview with Jesse Jackson, he walked over to me and asked if I wanted to join him for dinner. I agreed.

We sat at a large table with his camera guy and talked about what we witnessed during the day. My emotions were numb from the experience and it was good to talk to someone about the feelings we were having during the time we were there. I felt comfortable with him. He was extremely likable and had boyish charm. During our flight back to Tampa, he asked me if I wanted to go have a drink with him after the 6 o'clock news. I said yes.

From the first date I had with him, it was full-throttle fun. At first we continued our conversation about the Hurricane Hugo devastation, but we turned our direction to dinner and stepping out to dance. We laughed and joked around and in some ways I think we "trauma" bonded. I enjoyed my energy with him and each date the energy grew, until we were a power couple.

Since we were both in the media, we were doing things that most couples only dream about like attending media days at Disney World or having 4th row seats to the Rolling Stones concert, and getting backstage passes. We would always get into a restaurant or club without waiting in line or waiting for a table. I adored feeling important and the feelings I had when we were together.

I had so many fun experiences with him in the fast lane and we lived in a world of TV privileges. I fell in love and lived a "power player" lifestyle in Florida, full of advantages. A year into our relationship, he was promoted to a full-time anchor that required more time of his time and more focus on his career. He was five years younger than me and was in the peak of his career opportunities.

I can remember lying next to him in bed one morning and I looked at him while he was sleeping. He looked like a little boy and I was so happy. I heard these words in my mind,

"Separate yourself from him. He is not the one I have for you."

Surely that wasn't God speaking to me. This is a "pizza dream," I thought to myself. I looked at him again and thought, "I love him. I truly love him."

I heard the voice again, "Separate yourself from him. He's not the one for you."

This time I decided to talk back, in my mind, since I didn't want Anchor Boy to know I was having this conversation. "But, I love him." There was silence.

I began to play "Let's make a deal." What if I asked the mysterious voice a few questions?

I said in my head, "Well if I leave him, the one you have for me has to be funnier and better looking than him." I went on and on with my list of things I loved about my Anchor Boy but still argued by justifying my reasons for leaving him.

♥ *Love Beat*

If you are hearing thoughts that do not sound like something you would normally think but the words make good sense, it is your higher self, trying to get you to listen to higher wisdom for your good.

I glanced at him again and noticed he was waking up.

"Have you been awake very long?" he asked.

"Not really, I was just thinking."

He rolled over and kissed me and I found myself staying in the relationship for three more months. During that time, I noticed his eyes began to wander, but I continued to keep my focus on our relationship.

I invited many of our friends to celebrate his birthday with us at one of his favorite bars. During the festivities, I noticed one of the waitresses paying too much attention to the birthday boy. He was friendly to everyone, especially her. Towards the end of the evening, I saw her slip him something and he put it in his pocket. I asked him what it was and he told me it was just a business card. Of course I believed him, but I also had a knot in my stomach.

♥ *Love Beat*

If you have a gut feeling that something is not right, it is a good indication that it is your higher self-understanding. The intention of the situation is not for your best good. If you continue to feel that negative energy nag at you and it keeps you from having peace of mind, it is telling you to be aware.

The next morning, on his kitchen counter, were his usual things: keys, wallet and some change. I noticed there was a card folded amongst his belongings and couldn't help but look at it. It was the business card of the waitress she handed to him with a note on the back. It read like a coupon; "Good for one intimate bubble bath with me" and had her phone number scribbled down. I set the card down on the counter and asked about it when he walked into the kitchen.

He made light of it and said he thought she was just kidding around with him for his birthday. A few days later, I caught them together on an intimate date.

I couldn't believe it was happening to me again. We talked later that week and I broke it off with him. I was so hurt and felt betrayed. I got mad at myself for staying with him longer, when I was clearly not listening to my intuition once again. I had also found out that he had been seeing other people and that he had been cheating on me for the past couple of months.

My attachment to love and my fear of time made me blind to the warning sign, when it was revealed to me three months prior. I refused to listen to my higher self's wisdom to separate myself from him. Again I was absorbed by diluted love and I went home after our break up to lick my wounds. I sat in my big armchair and had a good rant about men.

I yelled, "Why do men always hurt me? Why am I not enough?"

I began to cry uncontrollably. I said, "God, if I had listened to you before would I have not hurt this much?" Then I had a revelation and a prayer, "God, if I have to hurt from this experience, please make it quick. I don't want this to drag on for years and I want to be happy again." I heard these words, "You must forgive him for what he did to you."

"What? Are you kidding me? I am the one who is in misery here. Why should I forgive him?" I asked.

"If you do not forgive him, you will be in bondage to him and your failed relationship."

It didn't make sense to my natural mind, but this time I tuned into what my higher self's wisdom (or my spirit) was telling me to do. I thought about it for a few minutes and I half- heartedly said, "OK, I forgive him."

A flood of tears exploded from my eyes and I began to be more pliable. This time I said it again with more of a heartfelt feeling, "God, I really do forgive him. He evidently didn't have the same feelings I did and I am sorry I didn't listen to you the first time. Please give me the strength to live this lesson and learn about forgiveness in the process."

As soon as I said that prayer I felt a warm energy come upon my body. It felt like liquid love pouring all over me. It was a tangible feeling of being wrapped in my father's arms. I didn't realize by crying from the pain of rejection, I was also releasing the dark energies of deception and betrayal.

♥ *Love Beat*

My intention and my prayer was to truly accept my responsibility for ignoring the warning to step away from a wrong relationship and to forgive his behavior toward me. When I finally walked away from the relationship, God used the situation for my benefit, even though the pain of it was meant to destroy me. It was also a lesson of forgiveness to propel me to a new level of understanding.

I stayed in my big armchair most of the day and part of the night until I fell asleep. I overslept and missed the next day of work. I didn't care about work. I didn't have enough energy to face my colleagues and needed time to sort things out in my mind. I decided to take a walk along the beach to regroup my emotions. I took a big deep breath of the ocean air and let out a big sigh. I began to get absorbed in the beauty of the environment and I could feel a peace coming upon my active mind.

I said to God and the Universe, "I am no good at picking out men and I am going to let you pick him out for me. The men I pick always hurt me. Is it me or them? Please show me what to do." I continued walking and talking to God in my head.

There came a point in my walk when I was enamored by my surroundings and I said to God out loud, "I love the beach! I love its beauty and magnificence. It reminds me of You and Your splendor. I am never leaving the beach until I get married."

I took a few more infused steps and I heard these words, "Who is your God... Me or the beach?"

At that point I realized that I had misconceptions about what I wanted in a man and in life. I had too many restrictions and too many fantasies about how love was going to come to me. I walked back to my beach chair, sat down and gazed at the ocean.

I said in my head, "I give up trying to make things happen on my own. I need You to guide me, God. There has got to be more to life than what I am living. I want my life to change."

I looked out at the ocean and I saw a small pod of dolphins. They were jumping and playing in front of my eyes for 45 minutes. I was amused by them and thought how free they were playing and being joyful in their environment. I thought, if only I could be that joyful and free. Deep down inside, I knew I could be free but I couldn't understand when I had love, I had no joy and when I had joy (which was self-created and work related), I didn't have love. I learned the rhythm of life in work and play, but I still couldn't find my love beat. I was never in the right place or it wasn't the right time or the right person.

A week later, some of my colleagues were going to a club after work and asked me to join them. I had spent most of my downtime healing my wounded emotions from my recent break up and reflecting on my past relationships, I was ready to lighten up. I agreed to go and when I walked into the bar to have fun, the first person I ran into was Anchor Boy.

A funny feeling came over me. It wasn't the usual butterflies that I got when I saw him, or the love that I felt for him; it was a feeling of neutrality. It was the feeling of him more as a colleague than an ex-lover. I was bewildered; there was no sting of hurt and no feeling of revenge or hatred. It was just neutral. He walked up to me and said, "Hey, are you alright?" and gave me a hug.

"Yes, surprisingly I am alright," I said with a smile. "I have forgiven you..."

He leaned over to kiss my cheek, as he did I said, "...and I am still praying for you."

"You are? Why?" He was puzzled.

"If I don't pray for you, who will?" I looked at him with compassion.

He hugged me again and from the corner of the bar I could see my friends watching the exchange, looking concerned. We broke our embrace and I turned to walk towards my friends. My friend Sandy came up to me and said, "Are you OK? I didn't know he was going to be here."

"Yeah, I'm good. It's weird, I don't feel anything towards him."

"You don't?"

"No, I really don't, but let's go somewhere else." I told her what had happened and how I forgave him. I also told her the lesson I learned.

♥ *Love Beat*

Forgiving is a powerful intention, when it is in its pure form. It breaks the chains of negativity that surrounds a failed relationship that would normally hold you in bondage. The continual thoughts that surround a break up are harmful energies that if left in your mind will cause you to bring them into other relationships and into your body. By continually wanting them to owe you an apology, you are setting an intention for someone else to pay a debt of forgiveness that they may never pay, keeping you attached to them. It is up to you to release that person and all the negative emotions that came through that bond in order to move forward. Forgiveness is freedom.

CHAPTER 3

Let There Be… Enlightenment

I started to look for something more. I began to look for my purpose. I needed guidance, after my breakup and my lesson of forgiveness. I tapped into my spirituality. It was in the quiet moments of my higher self's wisdom that led me to a church where I enjoyed making new friends. I found energy and the power of unity being around other spiritual people that could help nourish my thirsty soul.

I was still thriving in my career and felt blessed to have such a fun and interesting position, but I was still restless about not having a man in my life. In the core of my being I knew there was more to my life than what I was living, I was always searching for more.

It had been over a couple of years since my breakup with Anchor Boy and I was dating sporadically with no real prospects. I seemed happier when I wasn't trying so hard to be with a man, but I was never so aware of the time factor.

Society told me that if I wasn't married by age 40, then there was something wrong with me. I started to think, was there something inside of me that was preventing "him" from coming? I also started to worry about my biological clock. I asked myself questions about having children. Was it time to freeze my eggs or actively look for potential husbands? I really couldn't bring myself to do any of those things, because I remembered my prayer on the beach and decided to trust it would happen in God's perfect timing. I wasn't clear if I wanted children or not, until one day I settled the discussion in my head.

I was babysitting my friend's little 6-month-old baby boy while she went out for a date night with her husband. I had just finished giving him his bottle, when I looked down at him. He was the sweetest looking child with white blonde hair, big blue eyes and the rosiest round cheeks. I was rocking him to sleep watching him drift off to sleep and said to myself, "I will never have one of these, will I?"

I heard these words that spoke to the very heart of me, "I didn't create you to create children. I created you to inspire them."

A tear rolled down my cheek and I was immediately healed of watching my biological clock. I decided to thank the universe for showing me my purpose and for giving me a new perspective. I continued to pray for a change and believed one was coming.

One Sunday, I went to a service and sat next to a friend named Phyllis. Phyllis was a kind woman that I had met at the first service I attended. She invited me to many church activities and we always had brunch after church on Sundays.

This particular Sunday service I sat next to her and she said, "Hey Laurie, they are having revival services in Lakeland. Will you come with me?"

I really wasn't familiar with the term "revival" and didn't like the sound of it. It reminded me of the tent meetings out in the boonies back in the old days. I let her question go unanswered for a while because I didn't want to hurt her feelings. She asked me again, "Will you come with me?"

"Well, I'll think about it," I said in a noncommittal way just to keep her from asking me a third time.

She said enthusiastically, "They are having services all week and I was going to go Wednesday. Just come to my house and I will drive to the church!"

"OK, I will see what I have going on at work and think about going. I'll give you a call tomorrow."

Thinking about the revival was all I could do. I thought about it day and night until I couldn't think about it anymore. I called to accept her invitation.

Wednesday rolled around and I felt an excitement inside of me. I made arrangements to leave work early. I didn't know where the excitement was coming from, but I had high expectancy like the preacher had a magic wand and could mysteriously transform my life. I was hoping he could put me back on track of my Cinderella dream coming true.

We arrived at the church two hours before the service started and I couldn't understand why we were there so early, until I saw hundreds of cars already in the parking lot. I never saw so many people going to a church event like this unless it was a Christian concert or a special speaker.

It was totally insane and didn't make sense to my mind at all. There were hundreds of people waiting for the service to start and the new arrivals were scrambling to get good seats. We walked towards the front of the church and looked for seats near the front of the stage. It made me uncomfortable at first, but when I looked at the people around the seats, I could see the countenance on each face. Their faces were glowing with peace, others joyful and others in calm delight. I heard many outbursts of laughter completely filled with joy and others reverently praying at the altar. I was somewhat confused. I had never seen or heard laughter in a church, other than a joke or two from the pastor behind the pulpit.

Thirty minutes before the service, the church piped in beautiful praise and worship music playing over the PA system. Instantly people that knew the words began to sing along. I continued to watch the congregation prepare for the service and thought to myself, "There must be something big going on here." The only time I had seen that level of expectancy was when the Cardinals went to the World Series and certainly not in church.

Suddenly I felt my own excitement start to grow and instinctively hummed the beautiful music. Musicians came on the stage and played the same chords of the music coming from the pre-recorded music track and faded the song to play a new one.

The service was starting and people stood up to with the music. I felt goose bumps and the air was charged full of energy. It was a reverent kind of energy, holy. I could tell the people around me were being supernaturally touched by gratitude. During the praise and worship music, the divine energy was so strong it felt like angels were walking up and down the aisles.

At first, I was skeptical about what was happening, but I kept on observing. They posted the lyrics on a large video screen and people sang them out loud. A particular lyric resonated in my heart while I was singing. I could feel the walls that I had built up around my heart melting to the gentle music until I felt as if I was floating in a river of golden light. I was lifted into a spiritual dimension that was both peaceful and healing. It put me in euphoric state as I kept singing. I began to give thanks and was grateful for my life.

The music became a heavenly usher for the South African preacher who came out and belted out the song, "Thou Art Worthy." He sang in a booming voice that sent shivers up my spine. It was like he was leading us into the throne room of heaven, building upon the hearts and souls who were in unison of the music.

At the end of the song, it was so quiet you could hear a pin drop. It was also very reverent. I opened my eyes and saw people falling out of their seats and onto the floor. Some people started to laugh uncontrollably, while others were crying so hard they could barely catch their breath. I sat there and watched until the preacher told us we could all be seated.

Something strange happened to me while I was getting ready to take my seat. I noticed in the aisle next to me, in the visiting minister section, a man still standing up. It was if he was frozen in time and he had his hands raised in the air with his eyes closed. When I looked at him, I was mesmerized by what was happening to him. He began to shake and fell to the floor, and as he did, I felt a surge of energy like I had never felt before. It was tangible, peaceful and very reverent. It went through my body like a wave of golden light. I slumped in my chair from the weight of it. It made me feel blissful and humble. I didn't know if this was the power of God, but as the service went on, it got stronger and stronger.

Twenty minutes later, the minister pulled himself off the floor and sat in his seat. I watched to see what was happening to him. I still was skeptical about what was occurring in the service, but I was still intrigued by the supernatural experiences the congregation was undergoing. I attempted to listen to what the preacher was preaching from the pulpit. My last thoughtful intention was that I wanted to experience God like that minister did.

♥ *Love Beat*

Don't underestimate the power of intention and when combined with a heart-filled prayer, the universe will set into motion the chain of events that will manifest the intention into a reality. I prayed for change and with every fiber of my being I wanted my life different. I was tired of the way I was living and wanted to come alive in a new way. I desired to be spiritually awakened.

I closed my eyes and I felt a wave of Divine power come over me and my body began to shake. It wasn't like I was cold with a quick little shiver running up and down my spine. It was a rumbling shaking down to my core as if I was having a seizure from the inside out. I fell to the floor and couldn't stop shaking; it was like I was plugged into a light socket with powerful energy surging through my body. It stopped after a few minutes and I was able to get up off the floor. I sat down in my seat wondering what the heck had happened.

The preacher was talking about the joy of the Lord, he quoted a scripture in Nehemiah 8:10 it read: *"Go enjoy the choice food and sweet drinks, and send some to those who have nothing prepared. This day is sacred to our Lord. Do not grieve, for the joy of the Lord is your strength."*

It was the same scripture my mother showed me many years ago and I buried it deep within my soul. He continued to talk about how we were there to enjoy the fruits of the spirit and to be open to receive what the Lord has for us. He mentioned phrases such as "Be expecting" and "Be hungry" for God to "touch you" in a special way. I didn't know what any of that meant, but it must have resonated with my soul because as the preacher kept preaching, I began crying. I was crying for all the pain of my past and the pain of a future of a promise unfulfilled.

I didn't know what was happening to me, but I was beginning to surrender to the process. I didn't think about the people around me or how I looked. I didn't care about my ego. I was there with the intent to receive from God whatever He had to impart to me. In my mind I asked for wisdom, knowledge and for my life to change.

As I was thinking those thoughts, I started to shake once again. I was trembling during the service and the preacher came from the stage and walked down the aisles as he preached. During the service, he walked near people in the congregation and they would laugh, cry or fall out of their seats by the powerful energy that was in the room. I watched him walk near me until the energy involuntary forced my eyes to close and I was absorbed into it. I began to shake uncontrollably once more.

In my mind's eye, I remember seeing myself covered in chains from head to toe. I was a prisoner. I was feeling heavy from the weight of the irons that had me bound and all of a sudden the preacher put his hand on the top of my head and I heard him say, "Shake her, Jesus. Shake her!"

It felt like a lightning rod went through the top of my head to the soles of my feet, a powerful surge of energy gushed through my body. It caused me to fall out of my seat onto the carpet. The energy was so strong and I couldn't stop shaking uncontrollably.

In my mind's eye, I saw a huge hand lifting me up like a rag doll and shake me like a women shakes her rugs out to clean them. Chains snapped off of my head and I could see dust, debris and the links of the chains flying off me as the hand shook me harder and harder.

My thoughts where not about how I looked, but they were consumed by the motion picture in my mind showing me what was happening to me in the spiritual realm. It didn't matter to me what it looked like to others in the service, I just felt surges of Divine energy coursing through my body and seeing the chains braking off me. I didn't know what to do with myself, so I just let it happen. The more I surrendered my thoughts to ignore what was happening, the more enlightened I became.

♥ Love Beat

I was taken to a place in my mind where I became conscious of my own spirit and how damaged I was through my own thoughts and deeds. God was supernaturally shaking away old beliefs and hurts from my past that kept me from the life I wanted. All the dark love energy and old diluted mindsets were being cleared and released.

The Divine Love energy deposited in my physical body but my mind couldn't keep up putting me in a numb state. It was like a sedative before an operation and prepared me to go deeper into my spiritual experience. If I had resisted the process I would have been stuck in the same patterns, instead I surrendered without thinking it out. I gave up trying to fight and let the Divine energy flush away any negative experiences that were lodged in my soul. I allowed the integration of the new energy to unite my fragmented heart.

The shaking subsided for a few minutes and I could feel a heavy sensation where I couldn't move my body at all. It felt like warm liquid honey was being poured all over me, and I was resting under an electric blanket. The emotion I felt was love, Divine Love. It was a love so pure that I almost felt unworthy to believe I could experience it. It was the magnificence of a love that was humanly impossible to create. It was a love that reached the outer limits of my mind and my heart was so full, I could feel it want to burst out of me and spread to the world. I was filled with unspeakable peace and joy.

When the joy energy entered my heart, I began to laugh uncontrollably. It happened in waves, Phyllis told me. I would stop laughing. I would shake again and be very still and peaceful, until the process started all over again. There were no boundaries of time during this process, it was just happening and so very real.

I was taken on a spiritual journey where I had a conversation with God about my single state. I was pleading my case about not having a husband and remember the longing in my heart of a promise unfulfilled.

"God, please kill this dream I have of getting married and having a husband. Please make it die. I can't bear to live with it in me anymore." I could feel the emotion of grief and sorrow so vividly.

The words I heard went through the core of my being, "I cannot kill your dream. I AM LIFE!"

I shook uncontrollably once again and when I stopped shaking, I felt blankets and blankets of warm energy fill my body and fasten me to the floor. I was overcome by a love beyond measure once again. I felt cherished and adored like I did when I was a little girl. It made me blissful and accepted. I had the assurance in that instant that everything would be all right and my promise would one day be fulfilled. The revelation became so real in my heart that I began to laugh and laugh and laugh. That night I believe I was infused with the joy energy of the Lord.

The experience from the revival ignited my heart; people who had similar spiritual experiences with joy were calling the meetings "The Laughing Revival." I was curious about what had happened to me spiritually and became spiritually hungry for more. I wanted to eat up all the biblical principles and drink as much joy of the Lord every chance I could get.

The meetings were like going to a smorgasbord of different supernatural delights with a variety of blessings for me to tap into. I was awakened spiritually and my heart was filled with hope. My faith was growing and my pain of the past faded.

My past failed relationships were not in the forefront of my mind; I was looking forward to a future and learned the importance of peace, love and joy. I was able to tap into the spiritual realm by permitting my spiritual eyes to uncover the true desires of my heart. I discovered I didn't just want things for myself, but I had a deep-rooted desire to help people and serve the community.

Some days it felt like my head was in the clouds from all of the spiritual experiences and yearned to be under the anointing. That is what the preacher called the presence of God but I called it Divine Love.

Divine love is a pure spiritual love energy that transcends time. It is God's grace that set the Universe in motion. Angels, spirits and guides work behind the scenes to manifest your heart's desires. It is serendipity in action with all of its love, joy, peace, patience, kindness, goodness, faithfulness, gentleness and self-control. When Divine Love is working inside of you, you have the ability to love yourself in healthy ways. You are able to understand beyond your mind. Divine love dwells in you and you can tap into it at any given time and give it away to others.

For the first time, my spiritual eyes were opened to Divine Love and my heart recognized it was safe to feel it. With each infusion of Divine Love, I learned something new about myself and released something from my past. I became a student of the pure Source energy and learned how to incorporate biblical principles on a daily basis.

The Divine impartations helped my creativity at work and I came up with new innovative ideas and solutions. I was promoted to a senior producer and was flourishing in my position. I had favor with the government officials and it propelled my career in the community. I became a leader and innovator with youth and community outreaches. Being plugged into community service gave me a sense of belonging and satisfaction knowing I was making an impact on lives.

I couldn't get enough Divine love and continued going to the services. During a particular service, I had a heavenly encounter with an angel. I was singing and closed my eyes to get caught up in the moment. As I did, I felt an abundant energy pulsating through every cell of my being. I felt the hair on my arms stand straight up. I opened my eyes and I could see a radiant man-like being with shoulder length sandy blond hair wearing a white robe with gold piping. He towered over me. I really couldn't see his face, but he was holding a large golden vase. Intuitively, I wanted what he had in it.

In my mind, I could understand him and he asked if I wanted what he called the "oil of gladness" and I said, "Yes" out loud. He began to pour a thick golden honey-like substance all over my head and it dripped down on my face and onto my chest. It was a movie in my mind that seemingly played for only minutes, but in reality I was told it lasted for almost three hours.

While I was on the floor feeling the thick warm oil, my physical body was feeling something quite different. I was not aware of time or location. The only thing I wanted was more of the honey type energy. It made me feel euphoric and at peace all at the same time. I didn't try to reason it out with my mind, I just enjoyed it. When I did, I experienced a larger dose of laughter than from any of the other meetings. I could not pull myself off the floor and I laughed uncontrollably for hours. My laughter was hearty belly laughs that sunk deep into my soul as Divine joy and it was contagious. Everyone that watched me would be affected with uncontrollable laughter, not to point and laugh at me with judgment, but to collide with the spirit of pure joy. When I got up off the floor, something inside of me changed. I looked at the world with a positive new perspective.

♥ Love Beat

In the Bible, high priests anointed people with oil. What I experienced in my spirit was from the scripture Psalm 45:7 "You have loved righteousness and hated wickedness. Therefore God, your God, has anointed you with the oil of gladness beyond your companions."

I received a special deposit of joy energy in my heart that day. The oil of gladness was used to illuminate mourning. I had been in sorrow over not having a man in my life. I was mourning the loss of love and grieving over failed relationships. The oil of gladness erased the pain of those negative energies that were swirling inside of me and I walked away with my emotions healed and the fragments of my soul restored.

Going to the revivals regularly allowed me to shed fear and to expand my capacity to receive more of what God had for me during the service. Each meeting had surfaced an area in my past that I would be provoked to let go. I felt as if I was on a spiritual operating table with the negative parts of my past being gently carved out of my heart.

Laughter continued to be a sedative, keeping my senses numbed as I went through operation process of cutting away mistakes from my past and the negative energy around them. God infused me with His Divine Love and Joy and I wanted to know how to use it.

A few weeks later, Phyllis and I went to another evening Sunday service together. After a busy week of deadlines I was excited to be back in the presence of Divine Love. As the preacher spoke his message, he occasionally walked through the aisles and laid his hands on people at random and stopped to pray for them. I was secretly hoping he would see me and pray for me.

He walked by me stopped and said, "Stand up, Miss. I want to pray for you."

I looked at him and stood up. I slowly closed my eyes and directed my attention to having a surrendered heart to receive. He put his hand on gently on my head and said, "Show her the love of the Father, Lord." Then he blew on me and I fell down on the carpet of the church. It felt like a feather floating to the ground, so gently.

An electric sensation went running all over my hands and down through my body, reaching my feet. It was a very strong feeling of energy and I could feel it coursing through my body. In my mind I was saying, "I want to see Jesus. I want to see Jesus," but I heard the preacher say in a soft voice, "Show her the love of the Father."

In my mind's eye, I could see myself as a five-year-old little girl, so happy, twirling and laughing like I used to do. It was like I was watching a movie of myself. I stopped twirling and I saw a giant pair of radiant legs that were covered in a purple colored robe with gold piping. I gave the cloth a tug as if to say, "Here I am. Look at me!" A huge pair of arms scooped me up and sat me on their lap. I instantly felt safe and protected. I felt loved beyond measure; there was such warmth and compassion flowing through my little girl body.

I was being wrapped in a cloak of His presence. I could feel the love of the Father fill my soul and it gave me such joy and peace. Phyllis told me that I was on the floor in that state for most of the service. I didn't think about time or space. I was in suspended in time.

In a trance-like state, I opened my eyes and began to notice the ceiling of the church. I could see a golden cloud forming above the congregation and little droplets of fire were raining from the ceiling. I know it sounds ridiculous, but I believe I was given a glimpse of what was happening in the spiritual realm during this meeting. I remembered the same thing happened many years ago with my mother and me, when we were open to seeing into the supernatural realm.

My interpretation of what was happening was that Divine Energies were being deposited to those who were able to receive it. It was there to refine our hearts to receive spiritual gifts. I believed the gifts were for emotional healing, physical healing, restoration of the soul and knowledge. I later found scriptures to support my beliefs.

During the same service, a friend of mine was singing and fell to his knees sobbing. When he tried to sit down in his seat he fell out under the "Power of God." This was what the churchgoers called it when the Presence of the Divine filled your being and you couldn't stand up anymore. I was told he was on the carpet as long as I was during that service and with the visions that I saw; I knew something deep must have happened to his soul.

When the service was over, we met in the parking lot of the church and he was still groggy from his experience. I asked him what happened. I knew he was having problems in his marriage and was about to get a divorce. He told us that he had been praying about his marriage when a beautiful image approached him. He expressed the being was brilliant with vibrant colors of pink, green and blue. He said it was so magnificent he could barely look at it. Each time the image came closer to him it would shine brightly and it would take his breath away.

He asked, "Lord what is this?" He got no answer and the image approached closer towards him even more brilliant. Again, he asked, "Lord, please I have to know what this is! It is radiant and I am so drawn to it, what is this?"

He said he heard this in his spirit, "This is the spirit of your wife. This is what I see when I look at her, now you will see it too."

He crumbled to his knees while he was explaining this revelation to me. I could tell it made a huge impact on him and gave him a new perspective of Divine love for his wife.

With his new perspective, they never did get a divorce and their marriage was miraculously healed.

His story changed my perspective about my growing older, I had a new joy in knowing that I can have a man see me the way God sees me. I didn't have to worry about not being attractive enough. I would be attractive to any man who could see with his spiritual eyes. I reached the revelation that a combination of safe love and divine love would equal Forever Love.

The amount of emotional healing that came from the meeting was a turning point in my life and I began to feel loved and beautiful once again. I was restored from the pain of rejection and energized in a new way filled with hope. I knew at that moment that God mended my broken heart from the dark love relationships and showed me that I was worthy of forever love.

I continued to grow spiritually. My mornings were dedicated to getting up early enough before work, to take walks on the beach to meditate and pray. Each day I released the care of having a husband, yet my expectancy levels were still high. I knew in my heart God was working behind the scenes to make my promise come to pass.

But the years continued to pass and even though I was content, it was after my forty-fifth birthday when I started to get restless without a man in my life. I tried to tap into my spiritual faith and hope but this time it wasn't working and I tapped into my community service and joy to fulfill my need to be needed. I continued to be grateful for all the blessings of my life.

The old conventional ways of meeting men were almost obsolete with the emergence of online dating and it was becoming more difficult to find men in my age range who were not looking for younger women. If a colleague or a friend set me up with a date or encouraged me to go to an online dating site and I met someone, the first question I would be asked, "So have you ever been married?"

I would have to answer no and I was immediately judged as a "something must be wrong with her" type of woman or "she must be a psycho." To me it wasn't that complicated, I just figured out I was happier in my single state having a strong spiritual life than I was being miserable in forced relationship full of pain and dark love.

The years continued to pass with no sign of a man in my future, I was content with my life, but deep down inside of me was that unfulfilled yearning of forever love. While I was comfortably living in my "God Years" spiritual bubble, the dating world was changing rapidly. I quickly discovered that I was so spiritually minded I was of no earthly good. The reality of middle age dating and my religious beliefs changed the way I viewed looking for a man. I didn't look for guys like I used to, only concerned of the superficial traits and outer appearance in a catalog, I decided they could look for me.

♥ *Love Beat*

I learned when we get older, we tend to look at what is good for us rather than what looks good to us. I also realized that before my "God Years", I had been living under a victim mentality where everything that was happening was "to me" and I gave away my power in most situations and relationships. I had now entered a "by me" state of consciousness where I could control my situations and new dating reality with the use of my awareness of God (Universe, Source) and its wealth. I would set my intention and put it out there for the universe and God to manifest.

CHAPTER 4

Just Fabulous!

I began to gradually dip my toe in the online dating pool, despite the aging of my body. When I checked off the fifty-plus age bracket of my profile, I instantly felt the low energy of disappointment and low self-esteem creeping its way back into my thoughts. Even with all the emotional healing during the God Years, I still contained the negative feelings about my age. But I didn't let my age stigma stop me from trying to put myself out in the cyber- dating world.

Even though I was fifty years old, my dream of finding forever love never faded in my heart. But in my mind I couldn't help thinking, "Who would desire a fifty year old, never-been-married woman?"

Ageism slowly continued to haunt me and time became an obsession, with it came the pressure to stay young and reverse the signs of aging. I spent hundreds of dollars on anti-aging products, facial rejuvenation procedures and nutrition.

I became the "Queen of Creams" just to keep in step with the competition of younger women.

I couldn't remember a time when the dating game became such a marketing strategy. It wasn't that hard to get dates in my twenties; I enticed men with my body plus I had a body like J.Lo, but I couldn't do that now. I was middle aged and had a body like Jell-O!

♥ Love Beat

Way back in the deepest part of my soul, I kept the story of my friend's beautiful vision he had of his wife. That vision kept my hope anchored and grounded myself in a scripture found in Proverbs. Proverbs 18:22 says," He who finds a (true) wife finds a good thing and obtains favor from the Lord." So I prayed, "Lord make me a 'good thing' and a true wife!" I really wanted someone to see the love energy in my heart.

If the hands of time and the wrinkles on my face weren't enough of a reminder of my age, my body and the social stigmas were enough to bring the fear of time to my heart. I was going through menopause. Low estrogen caused me to feel like less of woman and between the hot flashes and night sweats, I didn't think I could attract anything but an 80-year-old dog. I fought back the emotions of becoming the sad woman with 100 cats! However, I didn't want to walk back into the victim mentality that I had in the past, (the "to me" phase). I learned to overcome that part of my life and began to appreciate my life just as it was.

Even though my blissful state of spirituality suddenly stopped with no warning, my resiliency forced me to market myself with a beefed-up profile of all my accomplishments, talents and witty phrases. I got in shape and put saucy pictures up to show off my new improved body and I waited for someone to notice me. That didn't work as planned either but I didn't let it stop me from improving my mental attitude about dating. I was determined to change.

I took a healthy approach of actively waiting by occupying my time with working on my inner self. I began reading self-help books, attended singles retreats, workshops and meet-up groups until I read *The Secret*. I discovered that I had a choice to make a change in my old patterns. I discovered I had the power to draw my husband closer to me by the Laws of Attraction.

I realized the way I approached the idea of a relationship in the past was with the energy of "want and fear of time" which caused every relationship to be distorted by dark love and my diluted ideas of love. I recognized I wasn't looking for a perfect man; I was looking for forever love, a love that was a combination of safe and divine.

With my innovative knowledge, I began to do my part to bring him to me. I began to pray him in. I made affirmations to attract him to me and made a list of all the qualities I wanted him to have, even the physical attributes. I commanded him to come forth like Lazarus from the tomb. I even had a mantra that I spoke out loud every day: "I am Fabulous at 50!"

I had entered into a "By Me" state of awareness. By realizing I could make things happen and create the life I wanted by the principals of the Law of Attraction. I was confident that my beauty came from the inside out, but knew a man wouldn't just land on my doorstep. I had to put myself out there in the cyber world if I was going to be found and be ready to receive him when he came into my existence.

I took my new spiritual views around for a spin on the new Christian dating sites. My screen name was "Fabulous, Fit and Fun!" I made a conscious effort to change the way I looked at myself. I created a profile that publicized my Christian qualities with only a few physical must-haves. I did want him to have all his hair and teeth! I focused on character traits and Christian beliefs, instead of the superficial things I thought were important in the past. I stood on the scripture in Proverbs about finding a wife, and kept praying I would be a "good thing." I didn't want to put myself out there as not being authentic, or not telling the truth about who I really was. I put enough information out there to be interesting.

♥ Love Beat

I learned if you put yourself out on the market as an imposter, you will attract imposters. I was beginning to understand that I was in control of my own attractions. If I wanted to have a fun energetic man in my life, I would have to be fun and energetic. My energy had to vibrate the frequency of what I desired in order to attract what I wanted. I had to be in harmony with the Universe to attract the thing that I desired the most. Simply put, if I desired to manifest forever love, I would have to resonate forever love.

Suddenly my dating tempo picked up and I was meeting quality men, but not feeling much of a connection with them. This was a new experience for me because I was a people person and could usually find something in common and build on it. The online suitors gave me new opportunities to explore different emotional energies around my intentions and my motives.

♥ Love Beat

By looking at my own motives, I could feel the energy of theirs. It was like looking in a mirror. If they were not upfront with their desires then I would check my motives and my attraction to them. Was I giving off a wrong vibe or feeling theirs? I could feel the energy of how they made me feel. If I was feeling distrust I would look inward first at why I was feeling this way. The answers were getting clearer to me if I checked my own motives first.

I also had a selective strategy for picking my dates. I started out seeing a picture of the man and would be attracted to a picture. It didn't matter who was contacted first. If I had an interested in his appearance, I would pull up their profile and read about him. If they had a good articulate profile, I would email them something witty and continue communication in email. If they had a very short generic profile, I would just let them go. I was a communicator and desired someone who could communicate their thoughts and desires easily.

Sometimes corresponding with emails was enough. I began to get a sense of their energy, whether it was desperation or big ego. I didn't want to spend my valuable time and energy on something that I knew could turn negative. I was biased to look for men who had a good sense of humor and liked to dance. I figured if I was willing to meet them, then I was determined to have fun with them.

I also had a healthy mental attitude for meeting men, with absolutely no expectations. In the past I would go on a few dates and the guy would be a prospect to walk down the aisle. In my new way of thinking, I would keep the conversations light-hearted and when I noticed time slipping away, I would break away from the date, causing them to ask me out again.

It was a formula that kept some men interested, because they felt good being around me, and it weeded out the ones with slightly different intentions. For me it was a chance to live in the moment and get out of the house. I just knew in my heart that one day I would go out and meet "him."

But sometimes my filters would be off slightly and a few imposters would creep into my life. Those men were more cagy and had a very strong charismatic approach with complimentary words and wanted to meet in more mysterious ways.

There were always "the signs." For instance, a few men wanted to meet me at my home, or only wanting to see me during certain hours of the day. I quickly discerned they were married and wanted to cheat on their wives. That was something that I never took part in. I wasn't willing to compromise my beliefs in order to have a moment of sex. I wanted a man who wasn't afraid of commitment and a long-term relationship.

My friends would say to me, "I can't believe it. Why aren't you married? You are attractive, funny and smart!"

I kept my sense of humor by saying, "It's because guys go for gorgeous, needy and buxom!"

I didn't lose hope, despite my sarcasm, but waiting was beginning to take its toll. I was deep in the throes of menopause and had to maneuver through some of my biggest health issues. How was I supposed to feel sexy about myself with all the symptoms of menopause? Not just that, but I also had to deal with menopause as a single, spiritual woman. Maybe I thought I could pray my way out of the situation. I battled words like "old maid" and "spinster" in and out of my mind on a daily basis, but I chose laughing about it instead of crying about it.

♥ Love Beat

There was still a tug of war going on in my mind. Do you really believe he is out there? Was it faith or stupidity? Whenever that battle would begin in my mind, I would meditate and think about my spiritual encounters with

God. I would instantly feel a peaceful energy come over me and see my way through the confusion. I figured if God created everything I can see and touch, He was able to put me on the path to find forever love. Instead of looking at what I didn't have, I looked at all the blessings I did have. It turned out that when I laughed about it, joy would flood my heart.

I decided for the first time I would embrace my age instead of run from it. I was in the best shape of my life, I was spiritually balanced, emotionally healed and professionally successful. Physically, I looked ten years younger (even without the Photoshop enhancements).

I finally looked at myself with acceptance instead of ageism. I knew deep in my heart that I deserved love and was ready to receive it. My expectancy was so high, I was like a child waiting for Santa on Christmas Eve! I was confident this was my year of meeting someone special and that summer I attracted someone who was as fabulous, fit and fun as I was!

My first date with Mr. Fabulous was at a well-known Italian restaurant. He told me he was coming from work and we could meet for happy hour at the bar. I got there a little early and I was feeling nervous, I really couldn't understand if it was excitement or nervous energy. My heart was beating so bad that I had to call Rose one of my Atlanta "Ya Ya sisters" to calm me down and help me sort my feelings out. (The Ya Ya sisters were Dyann and Rose, my best friends that lived in Atlanta. I met them when I was there doing freelance televisions shows.) Our group was a carbon copy of the ladies in *Sex in the City* with me being Samantha Jones. I was always dating the younger guys and always just walking away from diluted love relationships. I was trying to still muddle my way through my dating life during my forties even after my God Years.

"Rose?" I asked as she picked up her phone on the other end.

"Hey Laurie! What's up?"

"I'm here waiting for this guy I met online and I am really nervous about meeting him," I replied. "I have never felt like this before…what should I do?"

Rose was quiet and then asked, "Why do you think you are nervous?"

"I don't know," I answered. "He called me 30 minutes ago to let me know he got out of work late and was running behind. But my heart is racing and I'm not sure why. Maybe I think he's going to stand me up." I could hear the insecurity taking over in my voice.

She said jokingly, "It's probably you just getting cold feet to meet your future husband. Just toss back a shot of tequila that will calm you down."

"I don't want to be looped when he gets here. I'll just take some deep breaths and sip on my glass of wine," I replied.

Rose continued to comfort me with logic and as soon as I ended the call, I noticed a very tall man race through the doorway. He looked like he was crossing the finish line of a 5k race, hurried and out of breath. I recognized him from his picture and when he looked in my direction I waved at him and called him over.

When I saw him, my fears faded away. He looked just like the image of the man in my dreams, with a dimple in his chin. He was strikingly handsome and as he towered over the crowd I could see his salt and pepper hair approaching me. We struck up a conversation about traffic and he apologized for being late.

"Hi, Laurie! I hope I didn't keep you waiting too long."

It didn't matter to me what he said. His profile picture didn't compare to the man who was standing in front of me. I couldn't help staring at him, as he was a wonderful specimen of a man. I hoped I didn't start drooling at the sight of him.

He was 6'3 with an athletic build and his thick salt and pepper hair was fashionably styled. He was statuesque with a chiseled face and beautiful smile and his chocolate brown eyes were hiding behind modern glasses. I couldn't take my eyes off him, but could sense my insecurity and old mind pattern of "not feeling pretty enough" creep into my thoughts.

He ordered a craft beer and we began our conversation. I noticed during our stimulating dialogue, the novelty of his good looks wore off and he had a funny, intelligent personality.

We had a great conversation and as I finished my wine he said, "I'm hungry, would you like to stay and have dinner?"

"Yes, it is a good idea for me to get soppage!" I replied.

"Soppage? What is that?" He was puzzled by the word.

I began to laugh, "It's a word I made up when I need some food to sop up the alcohol. I call it "soppage."

"Oh, that's funny! Do you have other words?" he looked at me playfully.

"Of course. Maybe you will hear them sometime," I said as I flirted.

We continued our lively conversation during dinner, and after a bottle of wine and dessert. Before I knew it, the wait staff started gathering saltshakers and linens. We had successfully closed the restaurant, just talking and laughing with each other.

It felt like time stopped, there were no more years of waiting he was finally here, my "Mr. Fabulous!"

One date led to another and another until we were a couple. If I wasn't spending time at his place, he was spending time at mine. We enjoyed the Florida lifestyle, going out to dinner, cooking together, we went to the Buccaneer football games and other outings such as concerts and gallery showings. He was completely compatible with all the things I enjoyed and every time we were together it felt as natural as breathing.

During the week after work, we would meet each other to jog on the trails by the golf course or walk on the beach during sunsets. We were always sharing our workday war stories over a glass of wine or on weekends listening to live music and dancing. It was a magical relationship, full of laughter, love and hope.

About six weeks into our dating relationship, it dawned on me that we had never talked about religion or God. I was curious about who he was spiritually, since spirituality was such a big part of my life.

We were on the beach one evening enjoying the sunset and talking about our spiritual walk. He told me he went to a mega-church in Raleigh and how he had been a Born-Again Christian. He told me how he prayed to God about his transfer to Florida and before that he had been dating a woman who wasn't right for him. He continued his story by saying he came down to Florida to make a new start with his new job and was asking God to send him someone in his life that he could spend the rest of his life with.

He looked at me and said, "Two weeks later I met you. You are an answer to my prayers."

At first I couldn't believe my ears, was he talking to me? Can you imagine what those words meant to me? I was finally chosen at fifty years old! I was over the moon with excitement. I was thanking God under my breath and my heart was jumping for joy. I could feel the excitement course through my body like never before. I got chill bumps and I leaned over and kissed him. I looked at him and said, "Thank you. I feel the same way." He wrapped his arms around me and I felt his genuine emotion of gratitude. I looked up at the sky and my heart was beating out of my chest with possibilities and we began to talk about his daughters and his desires for the future.

At first I thought this was premature and that we hadn't even made love yet, but I was ready to explore a deeper relationship with him and take it to the next level. By his reaction to our discussion, he was in agreement too. Under a sunset canvas of blue, pink and gray, we left the bench we were sitting on, held hands and ran to the water's edge. We embraced in a kiss and splashed each other with cool water of the ocean. I was falling in love.

It was only a few weeks later when I accepted an invitation to take a long weekend trip for an oyster roast to meet his dad and other relatives in Maryland. Our trip to Maryland was educational. He always considered himself "a boy from the hood." I never saw that side of him until we were at one of his favorite places. We were at dinner having a cocktail, when he saw someone that he knew. He excused himself from the table and went over to the couple's table to say hello. I wondered why he didn't introduce me and felt unsettled about it. When he returned, I asked him who the couple was and he was pretty evasive with his answer. I pressed him a little more, because I was confused and he told me that some things were not for me to know.

I was puzzled with that response and instantly felt a negative energy surrounding it. I felt distrust. Later that evening, I confronted him about keeping secrets and he told me that it wasn't any of my business. The tone of his voice was demeaning and curt. I couldn't understand why he was acting the way he was and it angered me. I let it go, but it wasn't forgotten and on the way home I asked him about it again.

He explained that the couple was from his past and that there had been a severing of the friendship because of a bad business deal with his father. Mr. Fabulous was still upset about it, because his father suffered financial loss and was very ill. He said it was a long time ago and that he should probably just let it go. We talked about it most of the ride home and I couldn't help noticing the negative energy surrounding his temper. I helped him work through the negative energy by taking away the anger and coaching him through his pain. I realized at that point that I wanted to be a life coach.

Our relationship continued but not without its ups and downs. Mr. Fabulous' father became more ill and required an assisted living situation.

Mr. Fabulous was shuttling back and forth to Baltimore every other weekend and his workload was more demanding with more projects on his plate. Each time we were together, he begged for more emotional attention to help him through. He called me "his angel" and my kind heart and love for him couldn't resist his need to be nurtured in his desperate times, but his needs blinded me to my own.

It became a habit and he was drawing me into his life more frequently. I was constantly getting pulled into his family drama with his two teenage daughters, even work issues that came up were the center of our discussions. I became his Dr. Phil. He leaned on me for emotional support during his most turbulent times.

At one point I suggested we go to church together to encourage his faith in God and to implement more spiritual practices in our lives. We began a routine of going to church on Sundays and sitting together during the service was solidifying my love for him. There were so many times during my God Years when I dreamed of sitting next to the man I loved in the house of God.

My heart was open to receive love from him, but I wasn't exactly getting the love energy I needed from him. I noticed that he was getting more agitated when we were together. He began to be judgmental about certain areas of my life, and whenever I invited him to meet my friends, he would always have an excuse not to go. I noticed his temper flair up more frequently, but I ignored it. I would talk myself out of these behaviors by telling myself, "He is under so much stress, so don't take it personally."

I chose to be his oasis in the storms of his life and felt as if I was truly making a difference. In return, I was with the man of my dreams. I still felt blessed to have him in my life and I still felt the thrill of finally being in a relationship, but I didn't like the times when I felt taken for granted or judged.

💜 *Love Beat*

When you see a red flag and ignore it, it usually means you will see more red flags until they get your attention. It's best to assess the situation and see how it makes you feel. If you are feeling violated in any way, it is a sign of things to come and to get out when you can. If you continually resist the warning signs you are actually violating your own heart. You are setting the stage for dark love to play a lead role in your fairy tale.

It was ten months into our relationship when Mr. Fabulous decided he needed to leave Florida and move back to Raleigh, NC. He wanted me to come with him. We planned a trip together to see if I could get a media position in that city. From my experience, I knew Raleigh wasn't a big media market and that I would have to search very hard to find a position to meet my financial needs. I sent out my resumes and scheduled a couple of interviews. My excitement grew to the possibilities of being with him in a new town. In my mind, it was the equivalent of being swept off my feet to live my happily ever life.

Our first trip to Raleigh was exciting and new. He introduced me to his friends and we stayed at one of his church friend's homes. She was a woman that he met in the single's group, and she offered him a place to stay any time he was in town. Her name was Teresa, but we called her "Tee." Tee helped me get around town, showed me the cool places to visit while in town and we were building a very nice friendship.

Meanwhile, Mr. Fabulous was trying to do several things while he was in town. He had a house that he had rented when he moved to Florida, and needed to check on it with his new tenants. He was also interested in buying a new townhouse for when he moved back to Raleigh, since his home would still be occupied. He was checking in at work to see about his relocation costs and instructions about his new position when he returned. I, on the other hand, was going on interviews and feeling my excitement of a new life.

It was when I returned from my interview that Tee and I had a conversation about Mr. Fabulous. She had invited me to lunch with some of her church friends. Tee seemed to be an honest woman and was battling her own health issue of multiple sclerosis. While getting acquainted with her friends during lunch, she made a comment about a woman that we noticed in the restaurant and told me to "watch out" for her. I asked her to explain.

She told me that Mr. Fabulous was a womanizer and that she too was seduced by his charms at one time. She told me that the woman that we saw was married and Mr. Fabulous had an affair with her.

I couldn't believe what I was hearing and wanted to confront him about the accusation, later when we were together at home. That evening when Tee was at work, we had a long talk, so he could explain what I had heard. It was the second time I saw his rage over someone he perceived as betraying him.

He yelled at me and began to rage about Tee, calling her a monster and how could she tell such lies. He claimed she was jealous of me and that this was her devious way of trying to split us up. He was upset with me for listening to her lies and accused me of taking her side. He was so furious with her, that we packed our things, moved out of her apartment and into a hotel the next morning without saying goodbye.

When Tee woke up she called to apologize and also asked me to meet her in secret. My curiosity was aroused and I accepted her invitation. While Mr. Fabulous was out for the afternoon, she came and picked me up. She told me that when Mr. Fabulous lived there he had a friend named Eric and they would go cruising for girls at the local bars. Eric was married with an 8-year-old little girl and a newborn baby. She said the two would have a good time hooking up with women and brag about it at work the next day. She named several people to watch out for and gave me plenty to think about.

I was beginning to see Mr. Fabulous was not as fantastic as he first seemed to be. He was hiding an unsavory past. His safe love was becoming diluted with lies and misrepresentations of the truth. My feelings of distrust were getting stronger, but each time I confronted him, he convinced me that I was being silly and justified every one of his actions.

He persuaded me that it was all in the past and he was different now. He said that he was happy with me and that my love changed him.

I thought in the back of my mind, "Normally you would just run from this sort of relationship. But you need to start trusting more and you need to stick this relationship out and give him the benefit of the doubt. You are a Christian and you must forgive."

I forgave him every time he damaged the relationship with his disrespectful behavior towards me. I trusted him because of what he said on the beach when he told me I was an answer to his prayers. I believed in my heart that he was "the one." I had a low level belief that this was my last chance at love and I should make this relationship work. I could hear my dad's voice in the background of my mind yelling, "Laura Ann, don't fuck up this one!"

💜 Love Beat

By accepting Mr. Fabulous' behavior toward me and my limiting beliefs about this "being my last chance" to find forever love, I slowly began to give away my power. Dark Love energy began to infiltrate my heart. It caused confusion to my mind and a diluted ideal of what love was supposed to be. I fell back into the old belief that love equaled worry. So many of us want to be loved and we will settle for it any way we can get it. I was devaluing myself by accepting his dark love energy.

He had excuses for everything and charmed his way into my good graces. His behavior always made me feel off balance and uneasy, yet I still had a strong love for him. Was I being poisoned by his toxic behavior and addicted to his dark love? Or was I just addicted to his charm with his "Christianese" love talk that seduced my soul into trusting him once again.

Yes, on both counts. I was addicted to him. His love was like a toxic elixir that tasted like my favorite wine. I realized this wasn't the forever love I had been looking for. It was a twisted mixture of the darkest love of all, but I didn't care. I always gave him the benefit of the doubt.

I turned into the self-limiting princess that allowed a dark love Prince Charming, wrapped in Christian camouflage, sweep me off my feet with his seductive energies.

It was a combustible merge of too many negative energies and negative intents. Together, the negative energies blew a turbulent wave of confusion and fear over me, but we continued to navigate our way through a stormy relationship. With my rose-colored love glasses, I only saw the rainbow-filled sky, but there was darker and more turbulent weather coming that would cause a whirlwind of terror inside me.

Not too long after the Raleigh trip, his father began to decline in health and in his usual way, Mr. Fabulous recruited me to help take care of his daughters and help him with his dad. I enjoyed being helpful to him, but at this point I recognized how much I supported his needs by neglecting my own.

I was a faithful girlfriend and was very dependable. Meanwhile, Mr. Fabulous became more aloof and unresponsive to any request that I made. He always turned it around to help him in some way. I discovered the manipulation tactics he would occasionally use to get me to do what he wanted. It made me wonder what sort of Christian he truly was and I questioned his love for me.

When he was ready to move to Raleigh, he begged me to come with him. I couldn't see myself uprooting my life with his erratic love behavior, so I told him that I would prefer to get a job first before I changed my life. I figured this would be a test of my love for him as well. I wanted to make sure that he would be able to love me like I needed to be loved. So we said our goodbyes, while I helped him pack his bags.

We held each other so tight and kissed a passionate kiss. His eyes filled with tears and he said, "I'm going to miss you. I love you."

"I love you, too," I replied as I wiped tears from my eyes.

"You know you will be moving up here, don't you?" he assured me.

"Really?" I asked.

"Yes, I am coming back for you. Just give me until the end of the summer when I can get things straightened out. We can do long distance for a few months, right? Meanwhile, keep looking for jobs up here."

"OK, I will." I half-heartedly believed him and I was hurting inside to say goodbye.

We both got into our cars and he yelled out the window," Love you, babe. I will see you on the highway!"

"OK." I followed him out of his neighborhood and on to the highway ramp. I honked my horn at him and blew him a kiss. I could see him in my rearview mirror break down and cry. We temporarily parted ways with the intention to reunite soon.

CHAPTER 5

Winds of Change

E ach time he called, I was happy to hear from him. It seemed like our long-distance relationship was making us stronger. He was able to get control of his life without the frustration and he told me how much he missed me. I could count on speaking to him every night before bedtime and he would send a wake up text each morning.

"I know he thinks about me and misses me," I always thought to myself and it was the motivation to look for work in the Raleigh area.

My life in Florida without him was miserable. My job was getting more stressful and money was tight. My boss tried to falsify facts to get me fired and for the first time in my career, I was burnt out in television.

My supervisor and I would butt heads everyday over petty non-essential things and it was hard for me to motivate my staff. The studio was losing money and people were laid off each week. The lay-offs made us shorthanded, so our productions were cut in half. I was next on the chopping block, since I was the production coordinator. It felt as if I was having the life slowly choked out of me.

The stress was so intense that I couldn't sleep at night and I landed in the hospital for four days. While hooked up to monitors and IV's, I swore I was not going to let a job wear me down. I was going to actively change my situation by doing something else with my life. I began to research life-coaching schools to change my career. I was more active in my search for a position in Raleigh to be closer to Mr. Fabulous.

With a new attitude and game plan I managed to make it through the summer. I was able to cope by visiting him a few times. The first time, we enjoyed a Kenny Chesney concert with his daughters and the second visit was for another job interview. He came down to see me a few times as well, which helped us reconnect and keep the relationship alive. When we were together, it was so good and it just kept getting better. We had an appreciation for each other and I had my hope restored.

We each recalled the simpler times when we first met, walking on the beach and enjoying life. It would always be the magical place where we fell in love. But, I knew he had to go back. Each time, I would get a pit in my stomach that he was gone.

Labor Day came and he called me to tell me to start packing. He explained that he got a promotion and not to worry about getting a job. He would support us and we could move into his house. He was excited to move back into his home. The tenant was not renewing his lease, so we were free to move back in.

In my chaotic life, the news had me breathing a sigh of relief since my work situation was getting more tenuous by the day.

He said, "Let me get the house ready for you. Meanwhile, start packing your things and we'll put your furniture in storage for now. Pack up your clothes and your cat and you will have a place to land."

"For real?" I asked

"Yes, baby. I am coming to get you!"

I felt like he was the white knight coming to rescue me from the big bad witch, sweeping me off my feet and whisking me away to the foreign land to live happily ever after! My dream was finally about to come true at age 51!

I went into work the next few days with a positive attitude and set the date for my departure. I felt alive again and I began to count down the days.

It wasn't a big white horse, but a dark green cargo van that my prince charming drove up in, to sweep me away. He packed most of my boxes into the van and I sedated my cat and drove up to Raleigh.

I got a lump in my stomach, leaving Florida and my heart was beating from the fear of the unknown. I knew my life was about to change in a new way. I was leaving town to start a new life with the man that I loved. With each breath I took, I felt a magical, yet scary feeling.

We drove up to the driveway of a two-story home in a quaint neighborhood in Raleigh. It was a beautiful, peaceful setting of trees, children playing and greenway trails to take a jog. To me, it was now home.

The first few days seemed surreal to me, being alone in the house. While he was at work, I was busy nesting and unpacking boxes. I made dinner for him each evening and we would talk about the day. I felt as if I had turned into a little "Stepford Wife."

I was concerned about my cat, Riley. He felt displaced and scared. I tried to keep him as calm as possible, but he just hid under the bed in terror. Riley was my confidante for seven years. He was a Maine coon cat with long blonde tabby fur and big green eyes. He was beautiful, very large and very gentle.

Mr. Fabulous confessed that he didn't like cats and asked me to keep Riley in the garage. I explained to him that he was just scared and would acclimate in a week or two, but he continued to urge me to respect his wishes and keep the cat in the garage. Against my own better judgment, I agreed to put Riley in the garage at night. He was allowed to come into the house during the day. That was the first compromise I was forced to submit to.

For two harmonious weeks, we lived together in a blissful relationship. After work one rainy, chilly autumn night, he invited me to dinner at his favorite oyster bar where there was live music. I was thrilled to go out dancing and it was a fun place that I enjoyed going to in the past.

But when he got home, I had the old familiar feeling that something was not right with him. He blamed his aggravated state on his new job, but I could sense there was something more. He explained it would be good to get out to eat seafood, listen to music and to blow off some steam after a tough work week.

There was a great band playing and we were letting loose on the dance floor. We were laughing and having a great time, I felt our connection return and was enjoying meeting his friends and dancing. After our meal, the bar was getting crowded and he excused himself to go wash his hands. I saw him make a detour instead of coming straight to the table.

I noticed him talking to a blonde woman in a group of people for a long period of time. I walked over to him and he introduced me to the group, but not to the blonde woman. I was curious to know why, but didn't ask him until we were on our drive home.

"Your friends were really fun, honey. Who was that lady you were speaking to when you were with Eric; you didn't introduce me to her. "

"What lady?" He coyly inquired. He shifted in his seat a little.

"That lady with the blonde hair that was talking with you and Eric. Was she someone from work?"

He shifted again in his seat. I didn't know if he was shifting to see out the windshield or if he was becoming uncomfortable with the question.

"Yes, the whole group was from work. Why all the questions?" he asked defensively.

"Why so defensive? I only asked because I don't know many people here, so I thought you would just introduce me. That's all."

The rain came down harder and he strained to see out the windshield. He let out a large sigh.

I could tell he was annoyed. "I don't know why you have to interrogate me all the time. I was talking to people about a work project. Sheesh!" He grunted and muttered to himself for a couple of seconds.

I began to feel the mood shift in the car. It went from loving and caring to angry and annoyed. Sensing that I could get my head bitten off at any time, I remained quiet for the rest of the trip home. I also began to feel the sinister emotion of dark love enter the car.

Between my silence and his temper, the tension was building. I felt anxious, like a something was about to erupt. We pulled into the driveway and opened the garage door. As we pulled in, I could see my cat dart across the garage to find a safe place from the moving car.

Mr. Fabulous turned his head towards me and yelled, "You and your cat have to find another place to live!" His face became red and his eyes burned with anger.

I was shocked. "Are you serious?" I asked sheepishly.

"Yes, I have had enough," he muttered under his breath.

"I don't know why you are acting like this. What did I do?" I tried to plead my case and became very puzzled.

"You are wrecking my home and my life! This was a big mistake; there is NO future with you! I will never marry you and you are not even in the same league as me and my friends! I want you out of here!"

I sat with my mouth gaping and my eyes wide open. I couldn't believe he was speaking those words to me, out of the same mouth that said he loved me over a 100 times. Every hate-filled word he spoke to me, hit my heart like a missile. My body slumped down in my seat. The tone of his voice was belittling. His abusive words penetrated my heart and devastated my soul.

I began to panic, thinking about life on the street in a town where I knew no one. Fear gripped my heart and soul while he continued to yell at me until we were both out of the car. I walked around the car go into the house. He turned around to stand in front of the doorway. He looked stern and folded his arms.

When I looked up at him, he resembled a gargoyle guarding his post as he towered over me blocking the entrance of the doorway.

"Stay out of my house!" He screamed with his eyes blazing with fire. He took my arms and squeezed them at the biceps until they pulsated with pain. "You are not welcomed here!"

"But… my stuff is in there," I awkwardly replied and tried to break free of his grip.

He unlocked his grip and looked at me with disgust.

"NO! You don't belong here! I don't want you here anymore!"

He turned around and slammed the door behind him. The kitchen light turned off and I stood in the dark garage amazed at the turn of events.

Tears exploded from my eyes. How could this be happening to me?

I slowly melted on the stairs like a puddle of water landing directly next to the garbage cans. I started sobbing uncontrollably. I couldn't understand how my happily-ever-after could become the biggest mistake of my life. Feelings of rejection hit me like a tidal wave; I couldn't get the image of his angry face out of my mind. I flashed back to the time I was raped and was tossed aside like a piece of trash.

My heart was beating faster than a prizefighter before a big match, but I felt like I just received an upper cut from nowhere and was on the ropes, trying to stay alive. Instead of loving him with all of my heart, I was now afraid of him with every cell of my body.

Amongst the tears and trashcans, I sat in the cold, dark garage. I felt the soft fur of my cat, Riley, brush up against my leg, hoping to comfort me. He must have been hiding from all the yelling and finally came out to see what was going on. I picked him up and held on to him for comfort and warmth. We sat huddled like two harbored fugitives hiding out from the police. I had been physically and emotionally abandoned in that dark place with only my thoughts. I muttered a little prayer about keeping me safe when something illuminated my mind.

Only in the dark place of the garage was I able to uncover with the light of revelation, the things I couldn't see before. I would only allow myself to see the good in him and ignored the bad.

My desire to be loved was blinding me from the facts of who he truly was and his form of seduction and dark love. Mr. Fabulous lured me with his good looks and his hidden agendas; he charmed me into trusting him. I never saw his dark side because it was well concealed under his Christian sweet talk. I talked myself out of believing the bad things about him by justifying the good ones.

♥ *Love Beat*

Mr. Fabulous was no prince but he was charming. I had been seduced by a Charmer/Abusive relationship and I was ignorant to all the signs. I wanted love so badly that I fantasized a relationship that was idealistic. My "pick me "energy reflected his emotions to choose me as his prey. My emotions were enhanced by his ability to create a magical altered state of excitement by talking about a future with him. A manipulation so cunning, he led me into the trap where he could use his power over me and I would surrender to his. I was vulnerable, I wanted a relationship at any cost. I attracted a man who would give me what I wanted in a temporary setting because deep inside of me I still didn't feel as if I deserved forever love. Again I drank the fear and love cocktail and was suffering the consequences of dark love.

I was able to see clearly his strategy. His first tactic was to make me think we had many things in common. He mirrored my beliefs and knew just what to say and when to say it. He would sweet talk me into trusting him by making me feel guilty for not believing in him. He used God as a tool to force me to forgive him and he used affection and attention to close the gap when he felt me slipping away.

Once he had me under his spell, he began to devalue me and disqualified me as a suitable partner, because I was so flawed. I was no longer enticing to him and he would purposely sabotage our relationship by taking risks and trying to seduce other women. He would flirt with other women to keep me off balance and I made compromises until I gave up a piece of myself each time.

His final stage of manipulation was when he was bored with me (or the game). I would be discarded, so he would start the process all over again. It was a vicious deadly cycle.

Still hunched on the stairs with my cat in my arms, I buried my face in his soft fur and continued to think. I reflected back to the times we talked about God and spiritual things. I just assumed he was a spiritually mature Godly man, but I realized he was only mirroring my beliefs to "make the sale."

As I continued to meditate, I saw a light turn on in the kitchen. The door slowly opened and his silhouette was in front of the screen door. Riley hopped off my lap and ran under some open paint drop cloths.

I looked at him teary eyed, disappointed and afraid. At that instant, he became the enemy.

"It's too cold out here, come inside...," he said with little remorse.

I looked down at my watch, I had been sitting out there over an hour and I kept my gaze at the ground. I didn't want to be near him, I didn't feel safe anymore.

"... But the cat stays out in the garage," he said sternly.

I couldn't even look at him. "Let me get my things out of your bedroom and I will sleep in the bonus room from now on."

I gathered my pillow and my dreams and slowly trudged down the hallway to the spare room. I locked the door behind me, along with my fears and feelings.

Like a broken record, I played it over and over in my mind and tried to figure out what happened to make him snap or if it had been brewing all along. I thought about the rape many years ago and how those old familiar victim feelings tried to creep into my heart.

The damage to my soul was devastating: I thought I knew better, I thought I was an expert to recognize dark love. My whole belief system was shattered, my heart was destroyed and my spirit broken.

♥ Love Beat

By uncovering the hidden agendas of Mr. Fabulous, I was able to look at my situation as a learning experience and to gain greater understanding of the energy that surrounded it. I could see that I played an active role in the relationship by being addicted to the game of seduction. I could also see that my biggest fear was the fear of time.

The fear of time followed me like a dark cloud over my life. Through the world's assumptions of what is supposed to be at a certain age and my aging body, I realized I was in a deadline-oriented industry and my life revolved around time. The energy of never having enough time consumed my lifestyle and my life. I was constantly in a beat the clock situation, and my rhythm of life was never my own. By living in this type of energy I developed a life in the survival mode, always "wanting" and "never having enough."

When Mr. Fabulous came along, I felt the merry-go-round of time had finally stopped and I could enjoy life for a while. I created an ideal image for what my life was supposed to look like in my happily ever after, but it was far from the truth.

I should have stuck to my gut instincts about looking for forever love; instead of looking for my prince charming. This tactic would have had me on the right course of finding forever love. I also had to learn to embrace my biggest fear... time.

I spent most of my time during the winter months alone in the bonus room of his house. With most of my savings depleted, I was in no financial shape to leave. The cold barren trees reminded me of my heart and the fruitless journey I took to find myself still single, but now living as a prisoner of one big fabulous mistake.

Mr. Fabulous and I co-existed under the same roof amicably, but it was only due to my sacrifice of giving my cat away for adoption. It was just another piece of my soul he forced from me and I resented him each and every day.

As soon as he felt that I was gaining my own power. He would try his tactics to pull me in, but this time I was armed for battle. I had new knowledge of the game he was playing and I was silently planning my escape.

Mr. Fabulous continued to feed me his mixed signals of dark love during my time living in his bonus room. He continued his ranting against me with his harsh words and idle threats. He physically pushed me around and degraded me any chance he had. He cheated on me any time he could to make me feel unworthy of his love. I knew he didn't have respect for me and I was living in his domain where he made all the rules. I played along as best as I could, but I never knew when his rules would change.

I was able to repel his sexual advances and stand my ground. I discovered I had remarkable adapting abilities and would be able to equip myself by using an arsenal of imagination, faith and prayer to dig out of the mess I found myself in.

I had a strategy to escape from the unhealthy relationship with Mr. Fabulous. It was as if I were putting myself through a detox. In reality I was. I was shedding the polluted energy he immersed in me and filling myself with self-love.

♥ Love Beat

I had to have courage to admit that the relationship was unhealthy. It took his violent act of disrespect to open my eyes to the truth. He never loved me, not in a healthy way, but he wanted control over me. I had to understand that it was how he was wired and as wrong as he was in that behavior, I had to forgive him to move forward. I resented him for a long time, until I could forgive him. I knew I had to leave the situation, so I began to fill myself with the visions that I had about my life and love. I had purpose and tapped into it every moment I could. By putting purpose first, I was able to connect to my faith again and my hope came alive. I got stronger every day and I could see the light at the end of the tunnel.

My daily routine consisted of dodging him in the mornings when he got ready for work. Promptly after he left, I would listen to inspirational teachings and take a morning jog. I learned the art of meditation and used nature in the woods to heal my wounded heart. When I got back to his place, I would eat a healthy breakfast and lock myself in my room.

I would research jobs, send resumes and also looked for coaching programs I could attend. I had little money of my own and didn't want to ask to be supported. I was getting sporadic television producing projects to help me financially but it wasn't enough to move out on my own.

During an online search for coaching programs, I found a woman who was starting a beta life-coaching program funded by Duke University. I called her right away and set up a time to interview with her. When we talked on the phone, she was like a breath of fresh air. After an hour long conversation, she wanted me to participate.

Melissa was my master coach and a godly African-American woman who loved people. She was an educator and a natural coach. I would spend an hour on the phone with her every day, discussing the program and other life situations. We met once a week to go over the curriculum and my homework. I was beginning to feel the energy of my life shift in a new direction.

During the three-month immersion, I actually used the practices I learned on myself. I guided myself though my own inner healing and began to gain back my inner power.

Meanwhile, Mr. Fabulous was still trying to bully me into submission by taking "privileges" from me and threatening me whenever he felt I was slipping away from his control. He continually tried to lure me into his bedroom to convince me to give him another chance. All the while I recognized it was a game to him and a trap for me.

I kept the peace in the home by doing household chores and making him dinners, but I continued working on my inner journey and the way of escape. I came to a point of acknowledging the true nature of our relationship and I let go of harbored feelings against him.

It was at the end of March when I told him I was moving out. He was shocked because he continually told me, "Not to give up on us."

I recognized his idle words as just another form of manipulation and his good looks didn't affect me as they did in the past. He was love bipolar and had an unhealthy mix of dark energies that filled his house. All I knew was that I had to leave to survive.

In the spring, I graduated from my coaching program and I was now allowed to coach people. In order to get my certification I needed a set number of coaching hours until I could have my own practice. I looked online to find coaching opportunities and found a payoff.

I was finally able to make a graceful exit from my abusive relationship as a live-in nanny for a very rich couple who lived part-time in West Palm, Florida and part-time in Asheville, NC.

The woman had a three-month-old baby and she was overwhelmed, adjusting to her new life as a mom and business owner. I was hired to coach her and take care of her three-month-old while she cared for the two-year-old and tried to balance out her life. I was able to leave, save money and claim my life back.

Leaving him was the right thing to do, even though it was terribly difficult at times, because I had believed he was "the one." I instinctively wanted to give him the benefit of the doubt and desperately wanted things to work out. I wanted to believe him when he said, "Don't give up on us."

But the abuse would literally slap me back into reality, as a way of telling me to just walk away. That is what ultimately gave me the strength to leave. I knew any part of me turning in his direction would send me into a downward spiral into a pit of despair. I was not willing to go back there.

I did play the victim card occasionally. I couldn't understand how I could have not read the signs of dark love sooner. During the time I was working as a nanny, he would continually text, call or email me. He claimed he still cared and wished we could work things out. While we were apart, I discovered any type of encouragement from Mr. Fabulous had a spell on me. I continually "hoped" he would change and

I "wanted" a life with him. I would be back on the same path of "want" (a destination I didn't like to frequent). I purposely stayed away from him.

As time went on, I began to believe in myself again and found new opportunities and new friends. I was no longer a prisoner of his dark love. I felt my tempo change. I was free to explore and dance to a new beat. I was not just surviving, I was finally thriving.

By summer, I found myself strong enough to ignore the constant texts, emails and voice messages and strong enough to live my life on my terms. I had finished my coaching practicum, moved into my own place and rescued an orange tabby kitten named Monty. I was happy to have a furry companion back into my life and he gave me so much joy. It was a victory to be on my own without depending on anyone. I started to feel my rhythm of life return.

Summer was also the time when I found one of my best friends and a lifelong dance partner, Peg. Peg was an outrageously joyful person. I call her my "full throttle" friend.

I can remember when Peg and I first met; she actually picked me up at a bar. I went to a block party at a favorite hangout with my friend, Billy. We were sitting at a table outside watching the band, when Billy told me he was going to get us some drinks at the bar inside. I was "guarding" the table when a fun-loving energetic lady came over to me and said, "Can I set my purse here? My husband and I would like to dance."

"Sure!" I moved my stuff over and she set her red purse down on the table. She grabbed her husband by the hand and they both trotted to the dance floor.

The first thing I noticed was their enthusiasm and playfulness. It reminded me of how I used to be before all the bullshit with Mr. Fabulous. I can remember seeing them so happy and thought to myself, "They look like they are best friends."

The song ended, they came over to the table and introduced themselves. They were Peggy and Dave from Iowa, who moved to Raleigh back in 1990. They had a down-to-earth familiar Midwest vibe that I realized I missed so much.

Peg and I hung out at the table, deep in conversation when another great song came on. We both jumped up at the same time and said, "Do you want to dance?"

We laughed and went out on the dance floor to dance the rest of the evening. During our dance marathon, Peg lost track of her husband and I lost Billy to the crowd. We were having so much fun, we also lost track of time.

Meanwhile, friends from her group showed up at the table and she introduced me. They were just as fun as she was. When the evening ended, we exchanged phone numbers and made plans for happy hour the next week.

I was finally enjoying my life in Raleigh. Peg invited me to everything, pig-pickin' parties, group outings and football games. Peggy and Dave became my family and my safe love. I finally had laughter in my life again.

My life turned around. I rebounded in Raleigh with a great new position as a producer for a local television show. I had an active social life and was dating again. Before I knew it, I lived a Mr. Fabulous-free lifestyle for almost three years.

It was a couple of weeks after Thanksgiving when Mr. Fabulous called and begged me to have dinner with him before the Christmas holiday. He told me he had something important to discuss with me. He was really sorry for how he treated me when we were together and how good I was for him. My immediate reaction was that he must have some kind of superpower to sense when I was extremely happy and would swoop in and could screw it up for me, but I also knew I was equipped to say NO!

My curiosity got the best of me. I hadn't heard from him in such a long time, I wondered what could be so urgent. Something compelled me to listen to him. I figured it had been long enough that I could listen to what he had to say without it affecting me. I could have blamed it on the "warm fuzzies" of the holiday season or simple insanity. I really couldn't figure out why I wanted to see him, except I felt some unfinished business with us even though I had moved on. I convinced myself it was a meeting of closure, except when I saw him I still had feelings for him. I couldn't decide what those feelings were, but I knew they couldn't be denied.

He greeted me with a warm smile and a kiss on my cheek. I gave him a hug. I felt nervous, but not afraid. Was my heart still hoping there would be a future with him?

I didn't understand. I justified the desire to explore my feelings further. Had I truly forgiven him? I was totally confused. He talked throughout the dinner and apologized over and over. He told me that he was a changed man and I began to believe him. By the end of dessert, we were making plans for New Year's Eve together.

After the holidays, my life was traveling at the speed of light. I was busy working my dream job at the studio and busy with a new relationship with my old flame.

Everything in my life seemed to be going well and I was feeling like all the bullshit was worth it. But life had a way of throwing a curve ball in my happily-ever-after fairy tale.

It was early June when I received a 2 a.m. phone call from my brother in St. Louis. He called to let me know my dad had passed away. I was heartbroken; the man who brought me rhythm, love and laughter was no longer in my life. He was an entertainer who passed away with no fanfare, instead he quietly slipped away in the early morning hours. My mother never got to say goodbye to him, no one did. His heart finally just stopped beating and so did mine. I couldn't comprehend it. I spoke to my mother for hours and she told me all the details. I booked a trip to St. Louis to be with the family.

When I got off the phone with my mother, I called Mr. Fabulous to let him know the bad news about my father. He was comforting at first, but then he became distant. He told me in a harsh manner that there was no way he could hold my hand through my tragedy, because he was under so much stress at work. He didn't call or talk to me the rest of the day or the next. Again it was all about him. I recalled all the times I was there for him, the times I stuck by his side during his father's illness. How I was there for him until his father's passing, even going to the funeral to help him cope with all his family bullshit. I realized things never changed with him and probably never would, as many times as he professed his inward change. His outer actions were a giveaway. I started the grieving process, not for just my father but also for the loss of Mr. Fabulous.

♥ Love Beat

Did you know by continuing giving someone the benefit of the doubt is really giving them power against you? You have intuition that is trying to warn you of certain behavioral patterns or mind sets and every time you go against that intuition, you are setting yourself up to give away a piece of your soul. It takes inner healing and some people years to recuperate from the benefit of the doubt and the energy it takes to believe it. When you feel you need to give someone the benefit of the doubt, you are ignoring your inner guidance. It is best to keep your heart in check and say, "I forgive you for treating me this way, but it is something I cannot allow in my life." You will be empowered when you give yourself permission to speak your own truth.

CHAPTER 6

Dark Days Are Over

On the plane to St. Louis, I had a flood of memories of my father. The times he took me to the baseball stadium when I was young and how I met some of the award-winning producers and directors who worked with him. I didn't know that I would meet them again in my own career. I was so proud to hear the wonderful comments about my dad from famous broadcasters and former players.

I remembered all the great times I had listened to his music and I how much joy I had dancing to his Latin music. I thought of our Christmases together and how much we laughed over the years. I thought about how much I loved and missed him, and how I never got to say goodbye.

My mind instantly went back to my last conversation with him, telling him I would be home for Father's Day, since I couldn't come home for Christmas the year before. He was so disappointed that I couldn't make it home. I had started my dream job in a new studio and our first project was going to go on the air over the holidays.

I was sad about the timing and felt the energy of regret over "lost time" with him. I was sad that I didn't live closer to visit more often and I was sad he didn't say goodbye. I was just sad.

I flashed back to the phrase he said during our conversation earlier that week. He said, "I don't know, Laurie. I think it's time for me to fade-to-black." (It is a director's term to indicate the end of the scene or show. It is a transition to the end of something.) I think it was his way of telling me goodbye and that his time was up.

When I arrived at my mom's house, she looked scared and weak. She told me the whole story and how in the middle of the night he asked for some milk. She said, "Frank you know you can't have milk. How about some orange juice?"

He replied like a little boy, "Yeah, I want some juice."

She went into the kitchen and poured a little glass of orange juice, walked into the bedroom and said, "Here, honey. Here's your juice." She handed him the glass while he was sitting on the edge of the bed, waiting to take a sip.

"Thank you."

My mother slipped back under the sheets and heard him sip the juice. She heard him set the glass down on the nightstand and then there was silence. A few minutes later, she said, "Frank? Are you coming back to bed?" He didn't respond. She quickly turned on the light and saw him slumped over. She called 911 and located his pulse. He was already gone. My father passed away of congenital heart failure and my soul died of a broken heart.

💜 Love Beat

Grief, the energy around loss, is a tremendously powerful low vibrational energy. It is neither good nor bad it just needs to be acknowledged. You can can't afford to indulge it or deny it. It is an emotion of pain and that pain energy can get trapped inside of your body, particularly in your lower chakras. Its influence can bring you into a lower pattern of life where your entire vision has changed about your own existence.

Loss of a loved one can cloud your judgment into believing you have lost everything, including love. When loss is at that level and your primary focus, it can trigger depression and even death. Grief is the cemetery of life and you must choose to pull yourself out of the grave. Find a healthy way to help you grieve.

The months that followed were a blur. I was dead inside and couldn't function. My father was gone. Three months after his passing, my mom was diagnosed with uterine cancer, and three months after that I lost my wonderful new dream job. I had finally broken free of Mr. Fabulous, but had no love prospects in sight. I had no joy in me at all and I didn't recognize myself. I felt myself slowly disappearing in a whirlwind of grief, spiraling downward. The dreadful year of 2010 was the darkest point in my life.

I had scheduled a trip to St. Louis to be with the family and celebrate the Christmas holiday without my father for the first time. My mother had started chemo treatments, so I wanted to be there for her as well. I would be staying with her and could monitor how she was handling her treatments.

My younger brother Frank was eager to make dinner and celebrate the holiday to cheer mom up; he even paid for a ticket for me to be there with the rest of the family. Despite some family drama between Frank, and the youngest, Michelle, I was still glad to be with them. We each had time to catch up, enjoy some laughs, talk about the loss in our lives and most of all spend quality time with mom. In the end, everyone was glad to be together, especially me. I had nothing to go home to and knew that being with my family was not enough to get me completely out of the doldrums. My short five-day stay was a refreshing change to my deteriorating life.

I headed back to Raleigh for the New Year, but didn't have any major plans, except to face reality and try to figure out what I needed to do in the next stage of my life.

I woke up New Year's Eve morning with a shiver. I could feel the cold damp air throughout the house. It was wet and dark outside early in the morning and I heard the sound of ice hitting the glass window. I looked out the window to see what the day had in store for me. I saw lifeless barren trees with ice needles hanging from the branches. The frigid air began to seep through the windows as I heard the wind howl.

The clouds were low and dark, ready to explode with snow. It was officially winter in North Carolina and it was also the winter of my soul. Fresh off my trip, I realized I was still grieving the loss of my father, the loss of my job, the loss of Prince Charming. I felt like I had lost everything, including my hope.

I trudged into the kitchen to get a hot cup of coffee along with thoughts about how bad my life turned out and slowly sat down on my sofa. I wasn't ready to celebrate a new year, but I was willing to let the old one go. I turned on the television and stared at it. I was in a trance-like state and kept reflecting on the terrible turns my life had taken in just a few short months.

The weather stayed cold and icy all day, which reflected the condition of my soul. I sat in my dark lonely apartment sobbing as I continued thinking about all the loss. By the evening hours, I hadn't moved from the sofa. It seemed I was stuck. Stuck in a pattern of misery and I couldn't find my way out. I began to get angry about the twists and turns my life had undergone and I got on my computer to see if I could find my way out.

I checked my online dating profile to see if any prospective suitors sent an email. My inbox was empty and I felt like I was rejected by the whole world. I called my mom to wish her a Happy New Year and we talked for a little while. She tried to give me words of encouragement, but they bounced off of me as if I was made of Teflon. After speaking to her, I decided to watch a movie until midnight. I had no intentions of dressing up and mingling with friends. I didn't have enough emotional strength to fake it.

I stayed in my pajamas all day and successfully wasted the day by obsessing over my losses. My movie ended and it was getting closer to midnight. I walked into the kitchen to pour a glass of wine to accompany my sorrows and to watch the ball drop in Times Square on television.

"...3, 2,1 Happy New Year!"

I heard chorus of yells and fireworks around the apartment complex, but I wasn't happy. I wasn't celebrating. I just wanted to sit in my own pity party with my close friends, resentment and self-loathing.

After a few minutes of crying and feeling pathetic, I began to get angry. I felt a range of emotions rising up inside of me and I started screaming at the top of my lungs.... "WHY GOD WHY! WHY is this happening to me? I am so tired of waiting, when is it my turn?" I got some relief by yelling out loud and I yelled again, "WHEN IS IT MY TURN?"

The rage inside of me was like a keg of dynamite ready to explode; it was the emotion of anger that I had never felt before coming deep within my being. I was so fed up with my life without joy and fed up with wanting all the time. It made me so angry, I had to scream it out into the heavens for the Universe to hear me.

💜 *Love Beat*

The emotion of anger can be constructive or destructive. It has a powerful emotional vibration. When used constructively, it can catapult you from where you are to where you want to go. Anger can be the creative force to drive you forward to the next phase of your life. My desire was always to have something better in life but that caused me to stay in the energy of "want" or survival mode. I was frustrated living life that way and my emotions moved from desire to a vibrational emotion of anger. For the first time I embraced this emotion positively and realized I was the creator of my own experiences. All of the chaos in my life was crying out to be healed. Instead of running from it, I embraced it, felt it and let it go. Anger was the fuel that propelled me to make my life different.

Out of my mouth came the words of sort of a declaration. I don't even know where the words came from, (I had never heard the phrase before.) but just as loud as my "Why God why?" I yelled, "THIS IS THE YEAR OF PROSPEROUS CIRCUMSTANCES!"

I said it again and again. I said it three times and pointed to the ceiling as a declaration to the heavens. After I said it, I started to believe it. I looked up a scripture that I remembered about prospering. It was *3 John 1:2 "Beloved, I pray that you may prosper and be in good health, even as your soul prospers."*

I went to bed full of peace that night, I knew something had changed in my heart.

On the second day of 2011, I thought about my declaration and remembered the power of unity. I learned from my mom and the Bible that there was power when two or more were in agreement. What I didn't know was it is the God-like power of creation! There was only one person (besides mom) to share my crazy revelation. I called my friend James.

James was a man I had met online and had a brief romantic encounter when I lived in Florida. We stayed in touch even after I moved and our connection was still powerful and spiritual. He became a sort of guru to me when it came to learning new spiritual teachings. We would talk for hours over the phone and every time I hung up with him, I would feel like my soul was washed clean with new ideas, concepts and vitality. I nicknamed him "Hollyrock" because he was an actor trying to make his way into motion pictures. He was always my North Star pointing me in the right direction.

"Happy New Year, Hollyrock!"

"Hey Laurie, Happy New Year! Did you go out last night to celebrate?"

"No I stayed in. The weather was bad here, lots of ice. I didn't want to chance it." (I really didn't want to tell him I was miserable and couldn't bring myself to celebrate.)

"You?"

He replied, "I had a few friends over and we just chilled. It was a quiet night."

Then I asked, "I have a favor to ask you."

"Of course what is it?"

"Will you agree with me that this is going to be the year of prosperous beginnings for both of us?"

He quickly replied with a resounding, "Sure! Let's do it! I like this better than making resolutions!" His enthusiasm was infectious. "OK, I am going to declare it and then if you want to say something, you go ahead and say it!"

I bowed my head and said with my eyes closed, "When two or more are in agreement, touching anything, it shall be and so I declare this is the year of prosperous circumstances for both of us!"

He agreed and said, "So it shall be! This day it is set in motion!"

I yelled an enthusiastic, "AMEN!"

There was a powerful spiritual energy that I felt come through the phone. We both felt infused with faith and talked about it for close to 30 minutes. At the end of our conversation, we decided to update each other with our prosperous progress.

The next morning and all the mornings after that for the next couple of months were anything but prosperous. My circumstances got worse. My spirit may have been infused with faith, but my body could barely make it out of bed in the next few mornings. I spent most of my time reclusive in the dark lonely apartment. If someone reached out to call, I ignored it and just emailed later with a lame excuse. I didn't want to talk to people and didn't want people talking to me. In fact, I didn't want anything except for this feeling to change but didn't know how to change it.

To make matters worse, my usual birthday funk hit early, because I was approaching age fifty-five and never felt more like a failure. It was so much worse than my fiftieth! I couldn't find any work or projects and was not able to renew my lease on my apartment.

Four weeks after my visit to St. Louis, my sister-in-law, Sue, passed away and I couldn't afford to fly to her funeral. Death and despair surrounded me. It certainly seemed to me that the universe or God did not hear my New Year's declaration nor honored any prayers of agreement.

I began to feel the pressures of life from all directions. Again, thoughts of failure began to flood my mind and I was weak and rejected. I thought it was the lowest of the lows, but I was wrong. My life was about to get worse.

I heard a knock on the door. It was the assistant property manager, ""Here Laurie, I'm sorry." She handed me a piece of paper. "I will need your rent in the next three days, otherwise we will have to evict you."

I took the paper and looked down at it. "OK" Under my breath I said, "That's it, I'm leaving." I was totally defeated and I slowly closed the door.

I looked at the eviction notice and thought to myself "Rent, in three days? I only have enough money to put my things in a cheap storage unit. I really don't know what to do now and I don't feel like trying. The only thing I know to do is pack my things."

I took next the couple of days to pack and prayed for some kind of guidance. On the third day of my eviction notice, my apartment manager called and told me that she would not evict me until end of the month, since my lease was up anyway. That was the beginning of hope.

♥ Love Beat

Don't underestimate the power of your words. I was finally able to change the course of my life with the energy of anger and the power of my declaration. It was like prophesying to my old dry bones to bring them life. It was the breath of life to my circumstances. When James joined my declaration with a believing heart, the Universe had to obey the command. I knew the struggle was over and good things were going to happen to me even if I couldn't see it yet.

The few days before my 55th birthday my friend Jenny called and I decided to talk to her. "Hi Laurie! Happy early birthday!! What's going on? I haven't heard from you in a while, is everything alright? How's your mom?" Her voice was cheerful and bright. I didn't have a chance to answer when she bombarded me with more questions. I slowly answered them one at a time. Prior to that call, I was very protective and reclusive. I limited my communication to just my mother, an occasional chat with Peg or had a cyber-conversation with someone I met online. I wasn't very chatty.

I listened to her bubbly optimistic voice on the other line, "Let's do something to celebrate your 55th, OK?"

I really wasn't into celebrating anything, especially getting one year older and another year single. I certainly didn't want to bring her into my macabre world.

"I don't know, Jen. I am broke and no fun at all."

She said "That's OK, it's your birthday! Let's just go out and have some drinks. It's my treat and if you want to stay to have dinner, that's my treat too!"

I was reluctant, "OK, I guess I really should get out and celebrate life instead of dreading it."

She replied, "Yes, you can tell me all about what's happening when we're together. OK? ...and don't you back out of going, promise me...."

"OK, I won't back out. Where are we going?"

"Let's go to the new place that opened up down the street from my apartment. You can stay overnight, so you don't have to drive home."

I surrendered, "OK, why not?" I was secretly excited for the distraction.

I drove to her place, parked my car and climbed the steps to her third floor apartment. She lived with her boyfriend, Jay, and they welcomed me with a cocktail.

"Happy Birthday!" They cheered in stereo.

"Thanks, you guys!! You don't know how special this is to me, especially right now."

"What's going on?"

"Let's just talk about it later, I want to forget about my situation for a while. Can we just have fun tonight?

"Of course! This is about you today!"

The truth was that I hated celebrating my birthdays; every year that passed was just another year of singleness. I had been waiting my whole life for the love of a husband and every birthday it was just another year that it never happened. I was horrified at my current situation and was officially a hot mess!

♥ Love Beat

Even though I was healed from my emotional scars from failed relationships, I was shackled to the hands of time. Each birthday immobilized my thought patterns and ignited my "fear of time." I would get into a panic state about my age and it put me back into the emotional energy of "trying to survive." The "fear of time" caused me to make rash decisions or compromised my beliefs. It ruled my life and I didn't know how to break free from it. I finally decided to embrace it, acknowledge it and feel it, like I would any other fear. I celebrated my birthday by allowing myself to feel the fear of my future.

Despite my grim view on birthdays, I enjoyed the evening anyway. I opened up my mind to actually live in the moment. I found myself able to laugh again. I was thankful for the gracious gesture of my birthday celebration. I spent the night at their apartment and the next morning Jay made breakfast. After my first cup of coffee, I began to open up about my situation and the fear of being officially homeless by the end of the month.

Jenny could hear the fear of the future in my voice. "You can stay with us!" She was full of optimism.

Jay said, "There is no reason for you to leave Raleigh. Just stay here until you get on your feet. You'll see, it will all work out."

They each came over and hugged me. I felt like a charity case and I was, but I was also so very grateful.

"It's settled, you are going to move in here with me and Jay. You will just have to find a place for Monty since we already have two cats, but I think we have someone in the complex who will foster him for you. You can still see him every day. I will give her a call today and we can figure it out."

On March 3, 2011, I moved in with Jenny and Jay. I put most of my things in small storage unit; I sold my sofa and some other things for money to live on. I got a part-time job at Kohl's, so I could pitch in for food and buy gas. I began to start believing in myself again. The video production jobs began to trickle in and I slowly started dating again.

I felt hopeful.

Over the course of the month, Jay and I had several conversations about life and his relationship with Jenny. My coaching ears kicked in and as I listened, I began to hear something very familiar. I noticed the way he treated Jenny and I recognized it as dark love. In my mind, I knew Jenny was in for heartbreak, but I wasn't totally convinced. I could only hope that I was wrong, but the week that followed proved to be the mark that hit the target.

It was the first week in April, four weeks after I moved in with Jenny. I was working a double shift at Kohl's which included an overnight markdown night. I got home around 8 a.m. to find Jenny crying.

"Jenny, what happened? Are you OK?"

"Jay and I had a huge fight last night! He went to the gym and told me that he wasn't going to be home most of the day."

"So what happened?" I asked.

"He just blew up at me! He was told me he wasn't happy."

"Oh no, I am sorry, Jen, I said sympathetically. "He isn't happy with himself."

I tried to steer her thoughts away from herself and make it about him. In actuality, it was about him and his dark love.

She was devastated. Jay had convinced her to move to Raleigh while she was living in California. Jenny moved to Raleigh, exclusively to be with him. They had so much history together; Jay was Jenny's high school sweetheart and her first real love. They managed to communicate through the years and were both single, he wanted to rekindle the relationship. They had been living together for nearly two years when they offered me their spare room.

We both talked a few minutes over a cup of coffee and I went in my room and closed the door. My mind was wired from emotions and coffee, but my body was tired from working two shifts. I took a shower, hopped in bed, stared at the ceiling fan and fell fast asleep.

Jay came home and apologized to Jen. He told her he overreacted and they made up. I knew it was only a matter of time before there was another huge explosion waiting to occur.

The air began to warm and the dead branches of winter began to show little bright green buds. I decided I would run the Breast Cancer Awareness 5k Race in honor of my friend Rose, who was scheduled to have a double mastectomy close to the day of the race. I also dedicated the 5k to my sister-in-law, Sue. I wanted to pay tribute to her life, since I couldn't attend her funeral and because I needed to do something with purpose. It was my way of letting her go.

Since I hadn't run in years, I decided to start my training early on a greenway path near our apartment. I went out on the wooded path every day; the signs of spring were all around. The trees were alive with birds chirping and other animals scampering, excited about the warmer weather. I was getting my stride back in life too.

Every morning, Jay was off to work by 7 a.m. I got up right after him and ran the path. Jenny would wake up and write in her journal. After my jog, with my spongy-feeling legs, I climbed the steps to the apartment and by the time I got to the top I needed to cool off on the balcony, before I joined her for a cup of coffee to pontificate life.

Jenny was a kind compassionate woman who wanted to get her masters in psychology and we formed a unique bond of the artistic spiritual kind. We had met when we worked together at a digital arts college, and she was also a filmmaker in California. Jenny and I were good for each other; between my coaching and her psychology we were always encouraging each other and helping cope with our problems.

One morning after a jog on the path, I felt a stiff breeze and could the see the clouds quickly building up. I could smell the rain coming. I sprinted the rest of the way home, but something triggered sadness about my dad. I saw the dark clouds swirling fast and coming in our direction. I got to the apartment and out of breath, I raced into the living room just missing the downpour. Jenny was sipping her coffee and writing in her journal as usual.

"It's really blowing out there," I walked by her on my way to the kitchen.

"Really?" She asked.

"Yeah, it looks like there is bad storm brewing."

Little did she know I was referring to the turbulent whirlwind in my mind. I wanted to ignore my feelings, but they followed me into every room of the house. I walked into my bedroom and plopped down on the bed. The tears came rolling gently across my face. "Dad is really gone." A wave of sorrow hit me like a tidal wave. "I didn't even get to say goodbye."

Tears filled my eyes, as I glanced across the mementos I had of him. I constructed a little shrine with pictures, trophies and small tokens of his life. I surveyed the pictures and plaques of his accomplishments and could see he lived a rich, full life. I just couldn't believe he was gone. I sat on the bed for a while staring at the shrine and then slowly lowered myself to lay down. Hypnotized by the ceiling fan, I could hear the rain hit the window. I began to write in my journal: yelling within myself the big why.

"Why is my life so fucked up? Where is my joy? Where is the love?"

"Why is this happening to me? Why did dad have to die before I could see him again? Why did I lose my job and why can't I find one? Why do I live in Raleigh and just...Why?"

I could hear the raindrops pounding harder on the windows and I took a shower and fell fast asleep. I was emotionally drained from all the pontificating and all the worry.

Growing up in the Midwest, having tornado sirens in the springtime was a common occurrence. I could remember our family would go downstairs while my dad monitored the weather on radar. I had a flashback of him, as the weather grew worse and dozed off. I woke up to the sound of the wind howling and the rain pelting my window. I looked outside and I saw how dark and blustery it was. It reminded me that a tornado was on the way.

Our game plan for inclement weather was to sit in the most interior walk-in closet with our kitties, flashlights and portable radio. I decided to run across the street to the apartment where Monty was living and put him in his pet carrier to bring him with me. I knew he would be scared and I didn't want to leave him alone.

By the time I got Monty, the rain was coming down so hard it was sideways. I thought the smart thing to do was to stay in her apartment. I locked myself in the interior bathroom, got some blankets and sat in the bathtub with my cat. I had managed to find a pack of matches and lit the candle.

I felt the apartment building shake and rattle for a few minutes. The rain was coming down so hard, it sounded like bullets pelting the glass. The electricity went out and all I could hear was Monty's meows and heavy rain. After about 15 minutes, it was over. I took Monty out of his carrier and he ran under the bed. I knew the worst was over, so I walked back to my apartment. It was still raining and the downpour had flooded the parking lot.

Slowly people came out of their apartments to survey the damage outside, as Jenny and I watched out the window. There was flooding and several downed branches from the woods nearby. We watched the news reports of tornadoes hitting the area, even a few streets away. We were thankful we were safe. Meanwhile, the rain was still coming down and as the rainy day turned into night, I managed to keep myself occupied with old movies until I fell asleep.

The next day blessed us with a Carolina blue sky and the breeze was light and refreshing. I decided to lace up my running shoes and take my morning jog. I felt lighter emotionally, too. I didn't know if it was the clean air or the good night's rest. I noticed downed tree limbs and mud and debris along the path. I smelled the fresh air of the pollen-washed woods and breathed deeply in. I looked at the tall pines swaying with the cool breeze and noticed the sun peeking through the trees. Each time I would take a step, the sun would hit my face with its warm glow. I turned the corner to bright sunshine and heard these words in my soul, "YOUR DARK DAYS ARE OVER." I felt the sun beating on my face and closed my eyes for a second. I heard the words again, "YOUR DARK DAYS ARE OVER." Something in my heart jumped for joy; it was God and the Universe affirming what I had been hoping for when I made my declaration on New Year's Eve. Something good was going to happen for me.

I thought about the paths I took on my journey called life. I was living in a long winter, beginning with the loss of my dad. I did a recap of the loss in the past few months. Besides the loss of my dad, I lost the love that I thought I wanted (Mr. Fabulous), I lost my dream job working with students, I lost my place to live, I lost my sister-in-law and I lost myself.

💜 Love Beat

The tornado was a symbol of my life, living with struggle. I was in a cycle of struggle. I struggled with time, the lack of it and trying to out run it. I struggled to find love and struggled to love myself. I lived in the energy of struggle which produced lack in my life. I felt hopeful that the energy of lack was going to change into abundance, but I didn't know how it was going to happen in my current situation. My higher understanding allowed me to move closer to abundance energetically by having courage to believe abundance would manifest.

The turbulent tornado was a symbol that evoked change, whether I wanted it or not. The storm winds blew away dead leaves still clinging on a tree, which to me symbolized old thought patterns and mindsets that hindered me from growing.

The turbulent wind uprooted anything that was dead and collapsed anything that was weak in its path. These too were emotions built by fear, pain and anger, they turned into beliefs that don't serve us anymore. Storms are also the way a tree roots to become stronger; the force of the wind gives the tree knowledge to send its roots a little deeper to hold tight to the ground to withstand the assault. It is the same with faith. Trials give us a chance to dig a little deeper in our hearts to withstand the hard times.

I was living under the dark cloud of negative energy until the winds of the Holy Spirit blew into my soul. The power-filled breath of life was released through my words of the declaration. My faith co-created turbulence in the spirit and my blessings were about to break through. I realized I was a co-creator with the Universe. I was now entering the "with me" state of consciousness.

I realized that was God's way of stirring me up to believe even more and to let my faith increase to the point of trust. I learned my faith has to be bigger than my fear! I learned much from the tornado.

I was energized by the revelation and kicked up my pace. I ran through the woods. I could see the sunlight peek through the trees. I also looked at all the dead branches on the ground and the bright green buds on the trees. I could feel small seeds of hope being planted in my heart. I continued to look for other signs on the path; everywhere I turned was a symbol of a new season and of new beginnings. I picked a bright green leaf for my journal and stuffed it in my running shorts. I was convinced it was my time for renewal and I wanted the leaf as a symbol that I was entering a new phase of my life.

When I got home, I taped the leaf in my journal and wrote: "This is a symbol of the new beginning for so many things. This is for new growth, new relationships and new prosperous circumstances. Amen!"4/11/11

I began to feel a life shift. I had been creating a new profile for my online dating membership and every week I posted it for the world to see, only to take it down a day later. I had been playing a cyber-cat-and-mouse game for a few weeks before and after the weeks of the anniversary of my father's passing. I didn't know if I was strong enough to start any dating relationship while I was partially grieving. I wrote in my journal to comfort my aching, but hopeful heart. I was in a shit or get off the pot moment when I made the decision to date again.

♥ *Love Beat*

For the first time I was absolutely clear about what I wanted for my life, I wanted Forever Love. I thought I knew what I wanted before, but I was thinking it instead of feeling it. This time I was placing my intent with the guidance of Divine Love, knowing God, the Universe and synchronicity would make it happen in perfect timing. I made my intentions with a wholeness I had never felt before my soul was ready to receive. My intentions were in harmony with my heart and I was living in the vibration of it.

On June 14, 2011 this was my journal entry:

"This is the Year of Prosperous Circumstances and I believe I am a co-creator of my own life.

"I want to manifest the last love of my life. I always wanted to have a man in my life, so I want to manifest him this summer.

"I want a guy who has depth in him and understands spiritual principles, and practices them. I want a man with a sense of humor and is attractive physically especially to me. (6ft, at least with a dimple, if possible). I want him to have his own hair and teeth (a nice smile) and his eyes will twinkle when he sees me.

"I want to feel loved and cherished and have all the '5 A's.- Attention, Affection, Accepted, Appreciated and

Allowing' me to be me. I want him to find me physically desirable, even with my aging body. I want him to do little things for me like massages, cooking and taking me to local and exotic places.

"I want him to be adventurous and financially stable where he would be able to help me pay off debt (if need be).

"I want him to have his own home and to love Monty. I want that 'fit' I have been waiting for my whole life; the one who makes me feel safe in a storm and loves me like God loves me even to the point of great 'connecting' sex. I want it to lead to a permanent commitment and to live my life with my companion, lover and husband. I want this man and relationship to manifest now God.

"I call it forth, BRING HIM TO ME; Let me be found and let me recognize him and receive him! AMEN!"

On June 19, 2011, I put my profile out into cyberspace and received an email from David. His screen name was "Drama No Way" and my screen name was still "Fabulous, Fit and Fun." His email simply read: "I hear Pisces and Cancers get along well together."

I looked at his picture and thought to myself, "Oh no! He has dimples!"

Dimples were irresistible to me; I could say that I was addicted to them almost as bad as chocolate! Dimples got me in lots of trouble; I had many a bad date or stayed in a bad relationship all because of a dimple.

My theory about dimples was: the dimple would only show up when a person smiled. If I could see a dimple every day, I would know I am making someone smile and they were making me happy with a source of joy.

I read his profile, liked his "vibe" and became curious. I replied back to his email and wrote: "Yeah, I hear that too. I'm game to meet if you are."

He wrote back: "GAME ON!"

A couple of days later, he called to talk to me over the phone. He said, "Hey there, it's David from Plenty of Fish."

I was excited to hear his voice. He had a nice little Southern drawl, but by the next few sentences, I could barely understand him! "Can you date a Southern gentleman?"

His words were long and drawn out. It was the most southern twang I had ever heard! I pulled the phone away from my ear and said, "I don't know!" But after listening to his drawl for a little longer, I found his accent endearing and musical. We agreed to meet.

CHAPTER 7

Circle in the Sand

He was a tall slender man, and I spotted those dimples a mile away. I could say he was very attractive and very likeable. When we saw each other in the parking lot, he told me to wait for him where I was standing, and in true Southern fashion, he parked his car and escorted me to the door. He seemed very excited to see me and I smiled because he was a gentleman and I couldn't help looking at his dimples. I loved his chivalrous way of opening doors and pulling out my chair to sit down.

When we walked into the wine bar, the first thing I noticed was its charming ambiance. It had cozy nooks and inviting colors with earth tone colored pillows placed on the sofas that were peppered throughout the place. David and I picked a spot by the window with a view of the plaza, all lit up in globe lights. We began our lively conversation.

It was so natural and easy to talk to him. We could both feel a joyful energy as we shared a bottle of wine and ate appetizers. It seemed as if there was no topic off limits.

In the past, when I was interested in someone, my instincts as a producer kicked in and my dates would end up more like an interview or I would end up feeling like I had the "Big Ear" costume on, listening to the guy's boring stories all night long. I really didn't want to put David through that sort of scrutiny. I just wanted to have fun.

My conversation with David flowed very naturally; it was an even exchange of information with humor and wit. I had to know more about him. I asked him to play a game with me by using a letter of the alphabet of a word to describe a characteristic or quality he heard about himself or knew about himself. I gave him the first three letters and I did the next three letters. We played until we got to letter z. It was an interesting game and I was impressed by his willingness to participate. I discovered important things about him, without him feeling as if he was on a quiz show.

After we finished our wine, he wanted to take me to another spot that he frequented. As we walked to the parking lot to our cars he said, "You don't have to drive. Why don't you come with me? Do you trust me?"

"No!" but I hopped in the front seat of his SUV anyway. The truth was I felt something with him that I had never felt before, I felt safe. I didn't just see his outward appearance, I saw his spirit, (just like the man in church). I remember feeling so safe and happy with David. I instinctively knew his heart wasn't full of dark love, but it was full of safe love.

♥ Love Beat

The energy was palpable. There was something magical about our first encounter together. There was a comfort around him, but more than that I had peace in my heart. It didn't make any sense to my mind, but my heart knew it was safe. There was no fear, only peace. The choice for me was a simple: go with the flow or resist it. For the first time, I wasn't skeptical and didn't resist. I chose to live in the energy of the moment and to trust my intuition. I opened my heart to the possibilities and open my heart to trust.

Our second stop was a quaint bar with memorabilia and rustic décor. We ordered more appetizers and another glass of wine. Our conversation never died down, we were like two little chirping birds trying to out sing each other and just as lively.

When we finished at that location, it was about midnight. He said, "I have one more place I would like to take you."

"Oh no, I know where this is heading," I thought to myself. I was right; he took me to his place. He walked me through the house to the patio. He turned on music, brought me a glass of wine and we sat and talked by the moonlight.

A few minutes later, a neighbor three doors down yelled, "David, are you having a party?" His neighbor, Angela, walked down to his gate and opened it up. "Oh, I'm sorry! I didn't know you had company!"

I was delighted, "It's OK, come and join us!" I wanted to get the scoop from a neighbor's point of view about this man. She told me it took David three weeks before he emailed me. She convinced him to write me, but every time he tried, my profile would disappear. (This was during the period I played my cyber-cat-and-mouse game.) When I finally decided to leave my profile up and begin the dating process knowing what I wanted in a relationship, he emailed me.

I looked up at the moon on a very southern summer evening. The night sky was a mixture of trees and stars. I began to sway to the music and just enjoy the moment. Our conversation and dancing lasted until 3 a.m.. I was too tired to go anywhere, and David asked if he could call me a cab to go home. I declined his offer and after taking my contacts out of my eyes and putting them into a glass of water on his kitchen counter, I went upstairs plopped on his bed (fully dressed) and went to sleep.

The next morning I woke up and he was already downstairs making coffee. I yelled down the stairs, "Hey David, don't throw that glass of water away!"

He interrupted me and said, "Oh no! I forgot you put your contacts in the glass! I just dumped it out and put the glass in the dishwasher!"

"Oh no! That was my last pair of contacts!" I was wondering how I was going to squint my way home.

He was very apologetic, "OK, I will just have to get you new ones."

"No, that's OK. You don't have to do that."

"Well, you have to see and I want to do that, it was my fault." He pressed the issue until I agreed to his offer.

We made an appointment later that morning to get my eyes examined and get my contacts ordered. I had never had a man so thoughtful and so attentive to my needs.

Our relationship had turned into the Discovery Channel; I wanted to find out more about him and he wanted to find out more about me. We were exploring similar interests and I was beginning to agree with his first email that Pisces and Cancers really do get along great! We shared so much in common that I began to think, "He's just too good to be true." It was my usual self-sabotaging thinking I used to find something wrong with him.

It was a few weeks of dating David, when I got a phone call from my best friend, Linda.

"Laur, is that you?" She asked in her sing songy voice. (It was one of those funny familiar phrases we said to each other.)

"Hey gurl! What's up? I have big news," I said before she could get a word in.

"Yes, I do too. My dad passed away a couple of days ago."

"Oh, Lin, I am so sorry!" I paused, as she continued to tell me about the moment in the hospital room with him.

"I always liked Lou. He was a great man. Gosh Lin, he died almost the same day as my dad, only one year later," I explained.

"Well, that's why I am calling you. I want you to come to Ocracoke Island with me, so we can celebrate our fathers and meet Nancy and Ron." (Nancy and Ron were close friends who drove their RV to Ocracoke Island around the 4th of July each year.) "Laur, we can say our goodbyes to Lou and Frank together."

"I don't know, Linda. I have work and I don't have much money to spend on a trip." There was a million reasons I thought for not going, but only one good reason to go.

"Laurie, I need you with me. You don't need money. This trip is on Lou." She begged me to come with her.

"OK, I will go with you. I need to go, something in my heart is telling me to come with you. I will work it out."

"So what is your big news?" she asked.

"I met someone." My sadness turned into a big smile.

"Do you like him? What's the story? Can I meet him?" She bombarded me with questions and curiosity.

"Yes, you can meet him, in fact I want you to. I will try to arrange it when you are here. Until then, just let me know when you will be by to get me for the trip. I will let you know about work and we can iron out the details of the trip in a few days. Tell Nancy I'm coming!"

I hadn't seen Nancy in almost 20 years and our lives had certainly taken some twists and turns. She had three children who were all grown up and I had two decades of failed relationships and a successful television career. I was excited to catch up with her and spend time with my hometown friends.

That week, David and I spent time together. I told him of my upcoming trip to the outer banks of North Carolina. He told me about his family reunion in South Carolina. I was intrigued and wanted to hear more.

Every year for decades, his family united on the banks of the Edisto River to a river house on the 4th of July. He had been going to the river since he was in diapers, and it was a "can't miss" family affair. From ages eight to eighty-eight, generations of his family had been attending the family reunion. It was like tasting a slice of America in the little community filled with relatives, food and fireworks. David would be heading to his family reunion with his teenage daughters while I was away.

We had made our plans to see each other before our trips and I began to have stronger than normal feelings for him. David was my "Southern comfort"; he was sweet iced tea, biscuits and gravy and the "Carolina Shag." He gave me a deep-fried feeling inside and I was safe to be myself without judgment.

🩶 *Love Beat*

Divine love energy allowed me to see David's spirit, his essence, and I felt safe and cherished, even when he didn't say it. It was his actions and the way I felt when I was in his presence, I was at peace. My mind didn't race to insecure thoughts of myself as they did in the past. I felt safe, but I knew it was only a matter of time before I would start a self-sabotaging pattern once I felt comfortable in the relationship.

In my experience, I knew I could also feel safe in a relationship that wasn't good for me and I still had issues with trust. Before I could go any further in my relationship, I knew I would have to go deeper into myself to sort out some of my fears.

Linda called right before she left St. Louis, to let me know when she would be picking me up in Raleigh. I didn't expect her until later that evening. I agreed to see David before we left and arranged a time to meet. David and I had seen each other almost every day since our first date. I was either at his pool hanging out with his friends or he was at mine. It was finally beginning to feel like home in Raleigh for the first time without drama. I was enjoying a Carolina summer and learning a new rhythm of dance, the "Carolina Shag."

It was a couple's dance that most Carolinians did when they heard beach summer music and it was the first time I purposely learned someone else's beat of the music besides my own. David made me smile when he danced. I could tell he had gone to cotillions and debutant balls with his dance moves. He took me and twirled me around with a boyish grin and I felt like a schoolgirl at summer camp enjoying every spin around the floor.

It was about 9:30 p.m. when Linda pulled up; she was playing loud Latin music with her windows down. I came down the stairs from the apartment balcony where David and I were sitting enjoying a breezy evening under the stars.

It had been a while since Linda and I had a visit together and I was excited to see her. My heart was heavy for her and her loss, but seeing her gave me such boost of joy. She popped her trunk and pulled out her overnight bag and called me over to look inside, "Look what I brought!" I took a step behind her car and looked into the trunk.

My eyes opened wide and I said, "It's my dad's conga drum!" I heard from my brothers a while ago that she bought the set of three from him when she got into salsa dancing, but I had no idea she intended to bring one on the trip. I had a joy in my heart knowing that a piece of my dad was coming with me on this journey.

That wasn't all she brought. She had a couple of his Latin percussion instruments; the cowbell was in her front seat and bongos in the back seat. She told me she had been banging the cowbell all across the states, listening to Latin music as she traveled to Raleigh.

"You are one crazy lady and I love you!" I was shaking my head in disbelief because seeing her was just what I needed, a little taste of family. It wasn't only good for my heart, seeing Linda would help me sort out my feelings for David.

She knew me better than any human on this planet and I didn't realize how much I missed her. I choked back some sentimental tears and hugged her tight. When I introduced her to David, he was polite and funny.

David, Linda and I talked until midnight. It was time for David to leave, but while he walked towards the hallway, Linda fell in love with David's white and blue oxford shirt. She asked him, "Can we borrow your shirt?"

She looked at me and said, "Laur, you would look good in that shirt with your blue eyes on the beach. I have to get pictures with you in that shirt."

As soon as she said those words, David was unbuttoning to let me wear the shirt. I went in my room and grabbed a t-shirt for him and we laughed about it as he gave me a kiss goodnight. His shirt still smelled of his cologne when I packed it the next morning.

We got a late start that morning and after packing up the car, we made our pit stop at Starbucks for a quick bite. I had never been to the Outer Banks, but heard so many things about it. I was excited to go.

We started driving and Linda informed me that I was the DJ for the trip; she had various types of road music for us to sing and bang along to the beat with the cowbell.

Every song we picked would have a distinct rhythm and we could hear it and time our beats with the music. It was hypnotic and tribal. We began to yell out with each beat. We were making declarations to our fathers. We told them we were mad at them for leaving us. We yelled out what they taught us and what we loved about them. We beat the cowbell ten times for each thing we were grateful for, ten times for the names of people who disappointed us.

Each time it was my turn to hit the cowbell, I remembered something good or bad about my father and the other men in my life. It was therapeutic; the chaotic screaming of declarations and banging of the cowbell began to soften my hardened heart.

♥ Love Beat

The purposeful release of anger and fear by movement, sound or other vibrations, actually raises your vibration and shifts the energy to change the course of your life. The emotional energies begin to surface to your memory and that is the beginning of chaos in our inner self. We become aware of the hurt and the nudging to release the pain. When we move our energy moves and we begin to feel. When we feel emotions and surrender to the feelings of them, we are able to release the pain. It is a process and as you surrender to it, the layers of healing can begin to work deep inside of your heart.

If we hold on to the pain, resentment or anger, it will stay in our bodies and manifest in physical stress. When negative emotions are stirred up from a deep place of hiding that is a signal that your soul is ready to deal with the issue. You can ignore the nudging or resist it and it will keep on resurfacing in different times and areas of your life, until it is confronted.

You have to understand, if you allow yourself to go through the process of releasing or clearing negative emotion energies, you will have the transformation that you are longing for deep within your heart. It is entirely up to you to make the choice to let them go and surrender to the healing process.

By the time we got to Nags Head, I could feel a shifting in my soul and change was coming. We were singing to Adele, when Linda broke down in tears. She confessed she had broken up with a guy she was seeing and was touched by the lyrics of the song.

She said, "I don't know why I just cried like that!"

I could tell she still wanted to be with him, "It's because you still have feelings for him. You have to ask yourself why did you break up in the first place, is it something that can be fixed? How does he make you feel?" One question after another, I tried to help her sort out her tears.

She told me that he was not good for her and that she was being treated badly, but she still loved him and wanted things to work out. I listened to her justify his behavior and found that old familiar dark love energy lurking behind the scenes.

I knew this was something we were going to have to discuss later in the trip.

The music continued to play as we got closer to the ferry station to shuttle us to Ocracoke Island. Her drama-filled relationship with her Romanian boyfriend took a back seat to the beauty of the barrier island outside of Cape Hatteras. We stopped to get a bite to eat and snap pictures by the lighthouse. Her pain turned into pleasure, as we enjoyed the food, sunshine and water waiting for the next ferry to arrive.

It was close to 2 p.m., the sun was getting more intense and the line of cars was getting longer to get on the ferry. We waited our turn to drive up on the boat and felt the warm salt air hit our faces. We got out of the car, and posed for "selfies" on the top deck. I felt as if I was traveling to a land far away and could feel my anticipation build.

We arrived on the island and drove to Nancy and Ron's campsite. The RV had a large pirate flag hanging on the front and Nancy was sitting at the picnic table with a glass of homemade Sangria.

"Welcome!" She said with a big smile.

I had not seen Nancy for so long, but when I saw her, it felt like time stood still. She looked exactly the same. She got up and gave us both a hug. Ron came from behind the sand dune with a beer in his hand, "Come and sit with us down by the water!" We didn't waste any time. We shed our clothes to put on swimsuits and plopped into our chairs by the edge of the ocean with drinks in hand. It was glorious!

We had the best time catching up and deciding what to have for dinner. Nancy had made a snack for us and we decided to go into town later in the evening for dinner. Linda placed the conga drum by a sand dune and started taking pictures of it. Ron came up and was beating the conga and making silly sounds.

Linda called me up from the water's edge and said, "Laur, go put David's shirt on and I will take pictures of you by the sand dune with the conga drum."

Nancy quickly came over to join in the photo shoot. We all stood snapping pictures of each other with my cowboy hat and sunglasses. I put David's shirt on over my swimsuit and started posing. We were all laughing and having a great time.

"I want you to take off your swimsuit and just have the shirt on Laurie, David will love these shots!" She was in her photographer mode and I was giggling at the thought of taking off my clothes behind the sand dune.

It was primal and I really got into taking the shots. I pulled my curly red hair up over my head and posed sitting next to the dune with the ocean in the background.

"Oooh, that's a good shot. You should see your eyes with that shirt on and the blue of the ocean! It is gorgeous!" Linda gushed. "I am going to text David one of these shots for him to see!"

I was getting into it and Nancy chimed in, "Let me put your hat on and have some shots!"

Nancy began to pose with the hat on and we all took a "selfie" together. We each had our pictures taken in the cowboy hat and when they wanted to put David's shirt on I felt a little jealous. I kept thinking to myself, "Hmmm, that's my guy's shirt!

It was then I realized I liked David. I was falling in love with him and I was resisting the feelings, because I thought it was too soon.

I began to tell Nancy and Ron my story of how David and I met. It was during our conversation that I asked Nancy and Ron what made their marriage work. They told me that it was hard sometimes, but they were best friends and when one was down, the other one was there to lift them up. This always kept them in balance.

During the conversation, I knew I had to confront my past demons about men and leave them there on the island to stay. We enjoyed the laid-back vibe. I had no expectations. It was the pure freedom without being chained down by the hands of time that I enjoyed so much. The next day we went into town to stock up on food and booze, and spent the day hanging out on the beach and reminiscing over the campfire that night.

On the third day of our visit, Linda and I went to the beach alone. Ron and Nancy went into town to buy souvenirs. We placed our chairs on the most pristine beach I had ever seen. We both were processing our past relationships with our fathers, which brought about a discussion about men in general. Our conversation quickly turned into a discussion about the men in our lives, her Romanian ex-boyfriend and David.

I listened to her talk about this guy and I could recognize his dark love energy towards her; the catch-me-if-you-can game he was playing and how he enjoyed manipulating and stringing her along. It was heart-wrenching to see her agonize over an asshole like him. I decided to give her an example of how I learned to deal with bad relationships.

I found a piece of driftwood and drew a circle in the sand. I put one foot inside the circle and the other one out of the circle, I said, "This is how I am in relationships. I put one toe in at first and if I start liking the guy, I will put my whole foot in the circle. You see when I have a toe in, that means I am in the discovery zone, still finding things out about the person. If I like them I will put one foot in, but I still have the other one out so I can walk away if they do something that I don't like. You know if they have a bad temper or drink too much, my deal breakers. I just pick my foot out of the circle and walk away. What do you do in relationships, Lin?"

Linda got in the circle and stood in the middle of it with both her feet in. She said, "I go all in. I put both feet in and I stay there."

"What if he does something bad, can you get out? I asked.

She thought about it for a second and said, "No, I can't get out."

"Why not?"

"I just stay there, I can't get out. I can't get out!" She looked paralyzed and panicked. "I can't get out of the circle! I just stay there!" She was almost in tears, when a huge wave came and washed the circle away.

The wave was so strong, we both had to rush to pick up our shoes and beach totes from getting soaked.

We looked at each other and said, "There's no more circle! The circle is washed away!"

The circle in the sand was a pivotal moment for both of us. We discovered we had our own self-made boundaries when it came to relationships. We were captives in our own mind to the fear of being loved in a healthy way. Linda was afraid of being alone and would settle for the bad behavior of a dark lover's energies that would ultimately paralyze her and she would have no power.

On the other hand, I used my power prematurely to get out of relationships that didn't meet my expectations. My past experiences with men kept me from trusting them and I would make them go through a series of "tests" until they passed the test to qualify for my trust.

The circle in the sand stimulated a deep conversation that was bringing healing to our open wounds. We continued to flush out our emotions by talking about the lessons revealed. I realized I had too many boundaries and Linda didn't have any boundaries at all!

She didn't know how or when to step away from a bad relationship and was trapped between leaving and staying. Where I was able to fearlessly walk away from a relationship, if someone crossed one of my many boundaries.

Both of us recognized our behavior as old negative patterns that we wanted to break off our lives, something inside of me was stirring. Tears flowed from my eyes when I remembered something very vital to a woman's self-esteem.

I said to Linda, "I never heard my father say I was pretty." When the words came out of my mouth, I immediately saw myself as the little girl that looked in the mirror at my broken tooth.

"Ever since my tooth broke with the Time Bomb, my dad never told me I was pretty," I sobbed. It hit me hard and the emotions began to flow out of me.

The revelation of not hearing him say that I was pretty, led me down the path of diluted love at a young age. I equated his love for me by telling me I was pretty and when he didn't say it, I didn't feel loved by him and I didn't feel love for myself. I was constantly trying to find ways for his approval and in my adult life, I would seek ways of approval from the men in all my relationships.

It was as if a light shined down on the source of all my pain and rejection. It was at that point I realized that I was always trying to validate myself by hearing someone else tell me how good I looked. That was the exact moment my own heartbeat's rhythm stopped; it is when I began to run away from the joy that I knew as a little girl. My joy would return during my God Years, but as soon as I was in another relationship the joy in my life would stop once again.

♥ Love Beat

It was during the circle in the sand, when I realized that I was going around and around in my own negative patterns. I also came to the full understanding there was powerful energy surrounding the emotion of love.

It took the slow pace of an island to help me reflect and go back in time to determine the emotional energy that I absorbed from the rejection of my father and other men by being such an empathetic person. I could feel and absorb other people's energy and when it was negative, I wasn't equipped to confront it because I didn't recognize my own power to shake the negative emotions off.

The biggest revelation was that I still carried the negative energy in my body. It was causing stress, stomach issues and heartache. I wanted to be free and needed to let go of the past once and for all. I couldn't help going forward, surrendering to the process pulled me into the truth.

Our "Dr. Phil" moments unveiled the root causes of our past failed relationships and why we were attracted to such jerks. We came to the conclusion that we were addicted to dark love. We didn't realize dark love while we were in it, but slowly losing ourselves in the relationship, was always the end result.

We were blindly following the lead of a dark love dance partner and we were willing to give up our own power to be absorbed by theirs. We constantly justifying why we should stay in a relationship that wasn't working. We compromised ourselves so much that we didn't recognize who we were.

During our awakening, we decided we deserved better than that and we were not going to settle for dark love any longer. After composing ourselves from our painful stories, on a three count, we ran into the ocean to cleanse ourselves from our negative past. It was a symbolic gesture of purification and the beginning of our transformation.

Next, we each released negative emotions by speaking them out in the air. I let go of not feeling pretty and I purged the physical, mental, spiritual, emotional abuse from Mr. Fabulous. I purged all my lost opportunities to make good money in my industry and I released my heart to be open to love.

Linda did the same purging and a big gust of wind blew hard over us when she was finished. We talked about our fathers once again and cried.

We both felt a clearing of the old energies that kept us bound, but I felt a life shift. I knew something was about to change. We ran back into the ocean to wash off all the past negative emotions from those who wronged us.

♥ Love Beat

I felt a tangible shift in my energy after the final time I ran into the ocean to wash off my past. When I came out of the water, I was in such high vibrational energy that I could actually feel the layers of pain slowly dissolve off of my body. I looked at things with a new perspective. I had a new wisdom that had been hidden for many years. I was awakened and I saw through the eyes of love.

I tapped into the energy of the sea and the water was a conductor of all the abundance. Symbolically, water represents life of all things and I was being purified in my thoughts about love, cleansed from negative patterns and healed from the energy of past relationships. Even though I had major breakthroughs during the God Years, my time with Mr. Fabulous had brought new damage. I had to release the abuse and release the new emotions that were surfacing for me to deal with in order to move towards forever love. It took a higher vibration than fear it took courage.

Everything I did from that moment was a symbol of how my life was going to change for me over the course of the next few months. I was not only going to see with the eyes of love, but I was going to see love's energy. I was finally opening my heart to love and the possibilities of forever love.

Linda went back to her chair to read, while I walked on the beach. I felt invigorated and alive. Before the trip I had such heaviness of heart that I could not hear my own heartbeat. I was looking to restore my joy and listen to the whispers of nature. While walking the beach, I thought back to the first date with David. I continued to ponder my new relationship while I looked for shells. It brought a smile to my face as I thought about him and I found such beautiful large shells. I didn't have any way of carrying them and pulled the bottom of my cover up to hold the ones I had already picked up. When I looked at them I could see the sea's beautiful serene energy, but also the power of the surf. I wanted them as symbols of the peace I felt inside my heart and the thundering power I had working inside my soul.

The breeze on the beach was refreshing and renewing my spirit. I became alive to the sound of the waves and the smell of the salt water. I was back in my element, the beach.

Everything on the island gave me a new island girl vibe of vitality. I felt in tune with nature. I could sense the history of the island rising up in my soul. I felt more alive in that moment than I had felt in years and I decided with my heightened open state, I would enjoy each moment as it was given to me.

We gathered our things and drove off the beach to a picnic area close to the ferry station to meet Nancy and Ron before they got on the ferry. I showed off my shell collection to them both and we told Nancy what happened to us on the beach. She suggested we use the paints to commemorate our new freedom and we agreed it would sort of seal the deal.

Something magical began to happen; in my mind's eye I could see vivid colors surrounding the shell as if they were radiating a magical energy. The actual shell was a large peach, amber and brown scallop shell. It had a perfect shape tip on the bottom of the shell. But the colors I saw radiating from it were a turquoise and indigo blue so I painted those colors on the shell. I also painted the letters "OBX" 2011 (OBX is abbreviated Outer Banks.) on the inside of my shell I painted in deep blue the words, "HEALING AND RELEASE 2011."

After painting the shells, I felt like banging the conga drum. Linda agreed and pulled it out of the trunk. We began giving thanks out loud and hitting the conga drum. Another magical experience took place. I saw the heart-filled words spoken out loud, float up to the heavens and fade away. It was like I was watching a movie and each word resembled a light energy drift off into the sky. I was amazed at what I was witnessing.

While getting the conga out of the trunk, Linda noticed some old flip-flops she wore around the house. She thought it would be a great idea to paint them as a symbol of stepping in and out of the circle of sand and her new knowledge of how to step away from a bad relationship.

We spent the rest of the time visiting Nancy and Ron one last time and we hung out until the sun went down.

After we gathered up our artwork, we decided to stop at a Pirate Gift Store to look for gifts, then grab a pizza and go back to our motel room.

The Pirate Store was an incredible smorgasbord of booty! I was on a budget, but I couldn't shake my new groovy Island Girl persona. I wanted adorn myself with tribal attire and buy tribal looking jewelry to remind me of my island experiences.

Before the trip, Linda was living in a little bungalow styled home and was looking for beach décor to put inside of it. She took a shopping cart and wheeled it around the store, throwing pillows, wall decorations and pictures in it. I was scouring the sarong baskets to find just that perfect one that would have the perfect energy when I wore it. I found an anklet and ring that had "love" on it. It was a symbol for me to be reminded to be open for love. We spent over an hour at the store and had two carts of items. While Linda was checking out she asked, she asked, "Did you get anything for David?"

"No, I don't want to get him anything." I said.

"Why not?" she was puzzled.

"Because he might think I like him!" Linda looked at me still puzzled.

"But you DO like him. Go pick out a little something for him."

She was right, I did like him and I was just going back to my self-sabotaging behavior of playing games with my emotions. I began my search for the perfect gift. I just couldn't figure out what to get him but then I noticed the perfect gift under a pirate flag.

It was a beige colored ceramic tile plaque with a cocoa brown sea shell on it with cocoa brown words that read: "Be aware of your dreams. They just might come true." I knew exactly where it belonged, right on the wooden fence of his patio.

Linda and I took all our packages, pizza and went to our room. We were so tired, but it didn't stop us from sprawling the purchases on the beds to play show and tell.

She gave me a beautiful glass mosaic sea horse that had a beautiful turquoise stone in the middle of it. She bought a different color for herself and one for Nancy to commemorate our trip to the ocean together. We had our wine and pizza, sat outside of the motel room for a little while and got a good night's sleep.

We woke up early to participate in the local's Fourth of July island activities. We watched the raising of the flag ceremony, grabbed a croissant and coffee, and checked out of our room to watch the parade later that morning.

During the parade, Linda shared the story of her as a little girl who entered a Miss Firecracker contest. She didn't win because of a mix up and it must have made an impact on her at that age. I saw the pain of a little girl as she explained the story and I said, "Well, this is your year now! You are Miss Firecracker 2011!" I put some beads around her neck and we celebrated her freedom.

Miss Firecracker and Island Girl left Ocracoke Island changed and renewed, but there was still one more thing to do. We decided to have a burial ceremony to say goodbye to our fathers.

We picked a beautiful cove with sea oats and the setting sun reflecting on the water. We took the conga drum and placed it near the water's edge. I began to open slap the conga drum. I remembered a beat I used to hear my dad play when I was younger and tried to imitate it.

After playing few minutes of my father's beat, I could feel a primal guttural scream come out. I let it out as loud as I could scream. I played the beat faster and said, "I am here, Dad, saying goodbye."

I had a picture of him in my mind, taking me by the hand and walking me into the ocean as a little girl. I gazed at the sunlight hitting the water's edge. I kept slapping the conga drum louder and louder. I had loving memories of our times together and visions of us laughing. I continued to beat the drum with my loving thoughts. Out loud I said, "You gave me everything, Dad: rhythm, love and laughter." Then my beats got stronger and more violent and I started beating the drum in a chaotic fashion with no real rhythm at all.

"You also gave me pain and rejection." I said, "Why didn't you tell me I was pretty? Why did you compare me to your mother?" I struck the conga louder and just yelled, "WHY?"

My hands were tired and sore and my drum slaps became gentler and I started that familiar beat I started with and said, "I bury those negative feelings now! I send them deep into the ocean and whenever I look into the deep blue see I will now see beautiful memories of love."

I felt my beat getting faster and louder, Linda snapped a picture with her phone. I was getting caught in the moment, saying a prayer of thanks for all the things he gave me, including life.

All of a sudden my thoughts were no longer with my father. I could feel my heart beating faster and my beats getting louder and more sporadic again I had visions of Mr. Fabulous and I said out loud, "I let go of hurt and I buried the past in the waters of the cove. I released Mr. Fabulous and any lingering negative feelings I carried with me about him. I release everything that I had with him and anything that would try to attach itself to me to keep me from new relationships."

"Good bye old negative relationships of my past. You are buried deep into the ocean and when I see the ocean, it returns the energy of love to me."

I looked at the sunset with its golden glow dancing on the calm waters and said, "Good bye, Daddy. I love you." I took my hands off the conga drum and blew a kiss to the heavens. I was now at peace. I began to cry and turned over the conga for Linda to say her goodbyes.

Before she took the conga drum, Linda tied a friendship bracelet around my wrist and I put on my "love" ring and "love" anklet, to close the ritual, to complete the emotional clearing, and release of my father.

Linda followed me and took hold of the conga drum. She began to strike it with her own rhythmic beat. As she beat the drum, she thanked her father for all that he gave to her and said her goodbyes to the Romanian who broke her heart.

She purged all her negative beliefs about herself and the negative emotions carried with her from dark love relationships. She began to beat the drum faster and faster with each beat. I could hear a release of frustration and emotion. Linda was being healed.

She had a scarf around her neck and took it off to put it around her head. She started to get tribal with the conga drum, as I took pictures with her phone. She yelled out to the heavens, blessed her father and released him. She made a declaration about having new freedom as Miss Firecracker. When she was finished, she put on a butterfly tribal ring and I tied a friendship bracelet on her wrist. We hugged each other as the sun went down. We packed up the car and started our drive back to Raleigh.

♥ *Love Beat*

I felt invigorated and free from our "release ritual" by the water. Linda and I prepared for a magical trip and it turned into having our lives transformed. There was a freedom that the trip had for me, and the opening of my heart. For the first time in a very long time, I was able to receive. By the intent of have a healthy relationship with David, I was able to confront my fears from my past. I allowed myself to receive from the Universe all the abundance it would bring and I was open to forever love for the very first time because I loved myself. I walked away from the island feeling united in mind, body and spirit. I was finally in a place of harmony with myself and I was in the center of God's will.

A door of freedom opened when I began to deal with the hurts of my past. Purging the pain little by little, as it came up in my memories, was in perfect timing of my soul to be able to move forward in a new relationship. I was free of being manipulated from my past or from other people.

I couldn't navigate my new relationship with old tools, so I had to pitch out the old tools and make room for new ones. I had courage to start the healing progress, knowing it was a way to change my energy to a higher vibration.

Saying goodbye to my father was also a symbolic way to say goodbye to the other men in my life. All the things I learned from them good or bad made no difference. I was free of all of them by burying them deep into the ocean and transmuting my negative feelings into feelings of love. That was a turning point in my life and catapulted me to my destiny. I became aligned with my destiny and I was headed in the right direction to see it come into fruition. I was taking the path to forever love.

CHAPTER 8

Path to Forever Love

On the ride home, we talked about our adventure. We both had profound experiences on our journey. Linda decided to extend her adventure and drove to Florida the next day. My journey was just beginning on the path to forever love. I somehow felt different inside. My heart was opened to explore my relationship with David.

The next morning, before I went to work, I called to let him know I was home. During our conversation, he invited me to spend the weekend together. I could tell my feelings were stronger. He invited me to go to Topsail Island for his birthday later in the week.

Only four days after my trip to Ocracoke Island, this island girl packed her sarong and went on a road trip with David. During our travels, he told me how special this beach was to him. He had been going to the same beach with his parents since 1975 and it brought back great memories for him. He was excited to share with me the place that meant so much. I was so excited to have another trip to the beach; the ocean was always a place of rejuvenation for me.

We got to the beach later that morning and he set up the beach chairs and planted the umbrella in the powdery white sand. The ocean was rolling with waves, one after the other. The rhythmic sound of the waves washing up on the surf was a different sound than what I experienced on the island with Linda.

The waves at Ocracoke were turbulent and violent, but the waves at Topsail were rolling continual and the sound was melodic and serene. I didn't know if I was intoxicated from the ocean, love or the beer, but I was full of joy that day.

♥ Love Beat

After my trip to Ocracoke Island, my senses were highly in tuned to nature in a most unusual way. I began to feel the earth's rhythms that guided my footsteps to a path of forever love. Like signposts along a nature hike, I was being steered into areas of development. The elements of earth, wind, fire, water, animals and planets were all drawing me to wisdom to resonate with my soul and transformed my life. I was receptive to the still small voice of my inner wisdom by the abundant metaphors nature provided me.

I was happy to be with David on his favorite beach. After sitting on the beach all afternoon, we were able to check into our room and take showers to cool off. While I was in the shower, he walked to the liquor store and the grocery store.

It was my little secret to pack birthday decorations, decorative cups and a big "Happy Birthday" banner. I decorated the room and wrapped my gift (the magical tile I bought for him at the Pirate store in Ocracoke) and placed it on the table with a balloon.

When he returned from the store, he opened the door with a big smile. I could see delight in his face. I had another surprise for him; after my shower I had put on my sarong and was standing in the doorway waiting for him to pour me a glass of champagne.

The full moon magic cast her spell earlier on the day of his birthday. I could feel the lunar feminine energies. I was swept up in a goddess-like "vibe" and I was ready to give myself completely to him.

He had been such a gentleman and never forced his intentions on me, even when we felt such a strong chemistry. I wanted to wait until I had strong feelings for him instead of just having sex (which would have been good too), because I desired to establish something more than just the physical connection. I couldn't think of a better present to give him. "Afternoon delight" was an understatement to the connection we made that afternoon. His birthday celebration started out with a bang!

The bright full moon lit our path as we walked the beach hand in hand on our way to the restaurant that evening. We began to share more personal details about our lives. I shared some of the experiences I had during the "God Years" and he shared from times when he was a little boy growing up in Raleigh and coming to the beach with his parents.

The air was charged with a Divine mystique and we gazed at the moonlit waters and listened to the rolling waves. In that instant, I felt a soul connection weave pure love energy around our hearts that couldn't be denied. Love by the light of the moon, a Lunar Love inspired by Divine Love, and the nature that surrounded us.

♥ *Love Beat*

My new nature wisdom looked at the moonlit waves and told me they were a symbol to go with the flow. The rolling whoosh of the waves grounded my emotions and I wasn't afraid. Instead, I was very peaceful. It was from that lunar experience that I aligned my heart with my emotions. I began to breathe in spirit, but also grounded myself to the earth and the water to open the emotional part of myself that was closed off and protected.

The moonlight illuminated my awareness of my feminine side and in my heart I slowly began loving myself. During the lunar cycles, I found myself setting intentions, releasing old patterns and journaling my thoughts through the months. It brought me into rhythm with myself in a way that was comforting, grounding and peaceful. I could feel the joy in my heart building.

The next day we decided to for a jog on the beach. I had been a solo runner for most of my life, so running with David was somewhat frustrating to me. I couldn't keep pace with his long legs or the tempo of his jogging. I started out faster and he would be behind me. I slowed down for him to catch up and he ran next to me. I couldn't run at his pace and he would leave me behind.

A pleasant jog turned into a source of aggravation to me and I stopped running to ask him, "Do you like running in front, behind or side by side?"

He responded, "All of them."

I was more frustrated and puzzled, "What do you mean?"

He simply said, "Sometimes I like to lead. Sometimes I like to follow, but most of the time I like to be side by side."

It made sense to me and was pleasantly surprised that he was so insightful. I learned to run at a similar pace and we found our rhythm together. We enjoyed the day in perfect harmony, but later I received a phone call from Peg.

Peg called to invite me to drive to Florida with her to help her dog sit her daughter's dogs. We were going to be leaving Friday after she got home from work. I still had another week off and accepted her invitation.

This was our first official road trip together. I told David that she invited me and I was going with her. David and I were going to leave Topsail on Friday after lunch anyway. I would be home in time to do a load of laundry, just in time for Peg to pick me up after she got off of work.

David and I had another magical evening and Friday morning we spent having coffee relaxing by the pool. Our conversation turned into a discussion about religion and God he said to me, "I don't ever get visions or God dreams but I got one last night about you."

I asked, "Can you share it?"

I could tell he was amazed from the expression on his face and was hesitant to tell me. He saw me on stage speaking to thousands of people. He said it was so real and it made him have goose bumps when he spoke it out loud.

What he didn't know was I had the same dream many years ago during my God Years and my eyes filled with tears. Only God knew such a secret thing and I never told anyone else about it. I wrote it in my journal a long time ago when I had the dream and at the end of the journal entry I wrote, "And so it is! Amen!" 11/8/1997

At that moment, I believe that God gave David a glimpse of my spirit and in the same instant, I got a glimpse of his. It was a supernatural sign of forever love.

The purity of such a love is beautiful and fulfilling. It's the place where you are connected in a safe, unconditional way. A place where you are appreciated, accepted, given attention and affection and are allowed to truly be who you are created to be. It is that love that makes you authentically you.

For the first time in my life, my heart was able to recognize David as a man who would ensure forever love and for the first time I open to receive it. I prayed a man would see my spirit like God sees me and love me in an unconditional spiritual way. I wasn't just attracted to his dimples, I was attracted to his open loving heart.

♥ Love Beat

David and I were on a path of a higher frequency together, the vibration of forever love. We brought out the best parts of ourselves and together we could be joyful. I actually felt the merging of love and joy energies when we were in each other's presence. We didn't have to do anything, but be our authentic selves.

I had to ponder my feelings and settle my thoughts. My mind wanted to make sense of my relationship and I logically wanted to embrace it. I was open to all thoughts good ones and not so good ones. I asked myself the worst-case scenario and it really wasn't that bad.

I could sum it up in one word… Fear.

I remembered my mom telling me, "Your faith has to be bigger than your fear."

I asked myself one question, "Do you have faith that big?" Nature continued to give me the answers.

We walked on the beach one last time, packed up the car and stopped for lunch before our 3-hour drive home. When I arrived in Raleigh, I had just enough time to fill Jenny in on my extended trip plans and wash my beach attire for my next trip with Peg.

I felt as if I was reborn from my ocean adventures and there was a soothing of my soul. I was going to embark on the comedy leg of my island tour. I knew on a road trip with Peg, there would be plenty of laughs.

She didn't disappoint, right out of the gate it was a comedy of errors. Her husband Dave had to put new tires on her car before we drove to Jacksonville Beach, but they didn't have them in stock when he arrived. Peg picked me up and informed me that we had to make a pit stop to get the tires put on. The attendant at the tire shop told us it would be a 30 minute process and there was a Chick-fil-A next door. We decided to let the rush hour traffic die down and grab something to eat while we were waiting. She went to the bathroom, while I stood in line to order. When she returned she leaned over to whisper in my ear, she said, "Do I have anything on the back of my skirt?"

"No," I replied, "Why?"

"Well, I went to pee and my panty liner was not where it was supposed to be! I couldn't find it, so I thought it might be stuck somewhere else!"

I couldn't believe it! I busted out laughing uncontrollably and she did too. People were looking at us like we were crazy and I was imitating her walking in the tire store with her panty liner stuck on her shoe or on her sleeve while she was paying the clerk. We had to sit down we were making quiet the spectacle.

That's how Peg and I were together. We would get in situations that only we could, we played well together and it was usually a barrel of laughs.

Our drive on the moonlit highway was incredible; we traveled with the top down on her convertible, with music blaring and singing at the top of our lungs. We arrived in Jacksonville at about 1 a.m. and got settled in to get up early the next morning.

We loaded up a little red wagon with coolers, a sun umbrella, chairs and towels and rolled to the beach. It was a beautiful short walk to Atlantic Beach and I could hear the ocean still whispering my name. I was still thinking about my trip with David and had to fill Peg in on my new budding relationship.

"Peg, I met someone."

"Really? What's his name?"

"Take a guess," I said.

"Oh shit, not another David!"

"Yup, I answered, "His name is David!"

My new David was the 6th added to our group of friends and I was the second Laurie. As a couple we were known as D6 and L2 to differentiate the abundance of David's.

"Where did you meet him?" she asked.

"I met him online on 'Plenty of Fish'. I have been seeing him for a few weeks and just came back from a birthday trip on the beach right before you came to pick me up."

Peg could see the joy in my eyes as I was describing my new relationship; I gave her more details, while sipping mimosas on the beach.

After our conversation, Peg took out her camera and began to snap pictures. She said, "Turn around I want to get a picture of you!"

I put my head down and pulled a funny mustache out of my tote bag. "Just a minute, I have to put some lip balm on." I turned around and she snapped the picture.

She didn't notice the mustache I put on, until she looked at the picture. The wind had blown it crooked on my face and she snapped the picture. We looked at the picture and laughed so hard, we peed our pants. I looked like Peter Sellers of Pink Panther fame and I was doing funny voice imitations of Inspector Clouseau.

Our fun didn't stop on the beach in the afternoon. We rode bikes around town. I wanted to get another pin for my Island Girl hat, and we cruised by a Kmart. I asked to go in to look for a University of Florida Gator pin. We were riding in the parking lot when Peg said in a mischievous tone, "Do you dare me to ride my bike in Kmart?"

"NO!" I replied emphatically. (I knew Peg well enough that she would do it if I dared her to.)

A lady who was getting out of her parked car overheard our conversation and said, "I do!" That was all it took for Peg. She rolled to the automatic doors and when they opened up, she rode right into the store! I was right behind her and stopped to park my bike and hide my face. I watched her ride past the cashiers and say, "Do you know where I can find the umbrellas, it looks like rain!" She rolled right out the doors.

It would have been funny anyway with anyone riding through the checkout lines in a bike, but with Peg it looked like a scene from *I Love Lucy*. She was dressed in pink polka-dotted shorts with a white sleeveless shirt, riding a bright pink beach cruiser with a pink hat on her head. She looked like someone out of the 1960's!

Meanwhile, I was still on a mission to get my pin. I walked into Kmart with my head looking down at my fast moving feet. I could hear the cashiers buzzing about Peg. "Did you see that lady?" one cashier said to the other. "She asked for umbrellas and rode right out the door!"

When I came back through the cashier counter to pay for my merchandise, they were still talking about her, all the while Peg was outside thinking I had missed the whole thing.

I hopped on my bike and I heard her say, "You missed it! You missed me riding my bike into Kmart!"

"Oh no, I didn't. I got the aftermath of your actions! I heard the cashiers talking about you and I was trying so hard not to laugh in their faces! I have to call your husband, now I know what he has lived with all these years being married to you!"

I took my cell phone out and dialed her husband's number. I said, "Dave, now I understand what you have lived with all these years! I just experienced the Peg aftermath!"

I could hear him on the other end saying, "What did she do?"

"She rode her bike into the Kmart store!"

"She what? Oh dear God!" I told him the story and he laughed and said, "Welcome to my world!"

Later that afternoon, we decided we would keep the comedy "rolling" by going to a happy hour before dinner. We went to the center of town and found a quaint little main street lined with shops, boutiques and restaurants. I spotted a cigar bar called "Island Girl" and begged Peg to take a picture of me standing in front of the sign painted on the window. I cocked my cowboy hat and struck a pose.

After the pictures, we walked to a popular seafood place and ordered appetizers with a couple of margaritas. Peg reaching for the salsa and chips said, "Hey, let's call your David! I want to meet him!"

I was a little nervous about him meeting Peg (even though it was on the phone), this was a true test for David. He had already met Linda (my best friend) and with her help, I was able to sort out my feelings towards him while we were in Ocracoke.

Peg was different. I wanted her to like him. I shared so much with her while I lived in Raleigh that I felt like I needed her feedback. I valued Peg's opinion; she was honest with her feelings and open to tell me what she thought. If David couldn't hold his own with her, he wasn't going to make the cut!

I heard Peg was tough on boyfriends through the grapevine. I heard of tales from other girlfriends about introducing their new guy to her. The relationships usually ended a short time later. She admitted if they couldn't hang they were "OUT!" It was true, the year before I introduced her to Mr. Fabulous and we broke up a month later. I figured David was a good sport on our first date he would be able to withstand the bombarding questions from Peggy.

After a margarita, I had enough courage to dial his number and he answered, "Hey there!"

"Hi, I'm here with Peg. We are enjoying happy hour and I wanted to say, Hi!"

As soon as I finished my sentence, Peg grabbed my cell phone from my hand, she said, "Hey David, did you know I have a license to peddle pussy in Florida?" I think she wanted to put him in shock first before the third degree and I grabbed the phone away from her.

David said, "I heard that joke already!"

I replied, "NO, you don't understand! She really did peddle her pussy in Florida! She rode her bike into Kmart!"

I elaborated on the details of our story with Peg grabbing the phone out of my hand once again. She was laughing and finished her side of the story. He must have indulged her with a conversation. A few minutes later, she handed me the phone.

"Hi again, so what did she say to you?" I asked.

"It was nothing. She was just kidding around. Nothing I couldn't handle. She's funny!"

"Yeah, well thanks for being such a good sport. I will let you know when I come home next week, OK?"

"Sure. Have a good time!"

"I will. See you soon!" I hung up from him and said to her, "Peg, I cannot believe you grabbed the phone from my hand!"

"He was nice, I liked him! I can't wait to meet him in person," she said.

After our happy hour antics, we walked down main street and began shopping for little trinkets. We walked by "Island Girl" bar again and this time went in for a drink and cigar. I picked out my favorite stogie and lit up. Peg ordered a mixed drink and began talking to the person next to her.

A few short minutes later, she introduced me to a group of five that had been there most of the evening. She found out they were from the same town in Iowa. Needless to say, we closed down the bar and found our way home.

The next morning I woke up restless and needed to take a jog on the beach. I laced up my running shoes, meanwhile Peg was already out walking the dogs.

I was a little hung over, not so much from the margaritas but from all the thoughts about David floating around in my head. I wanted some alone time to sort it out. I couldn't understand why I had such strong feelings for him in such a short amount of time.

My mind was trying to talk me out of what a great guy he was and I just should wait for "the other shoe to drop." Back and forth like a tennis match, my mind would think about great things about David and would contradict the happy thoughts by trying to talk me out of my feelings.

I walked out to a rocky jetty that was past the harbor of my running path. I wanted to just have a quiet time of meditation and gaze at the calming ocean waters. I had peaceful music playing on my iPod and I was deep into my thoughts.

I heard a funny sound, like a blow-hole clearing water. I looked at the water and there was a dolphin staring up at me. I looked at his eye and the big smile on his face. He was curious looking at me and he opened his mouth as it to be greeting me and to say, "Welcome to my world!"

I didn't know what to do but to watch him with the beautiful music playing in my ear buds. I looked just beyond the jetty and there was another dolphin. I slowly stood up and balanced myself on the rocks to walk to the end of the jetty. As I did, the dolphin followed me out to the deeper waters where the other dolphin was swimming. I slowly sat down on the very last rock and watched them play together for at least 20 solid minutes. It was a delight and I smiled to see such a display of nature.

Watching the dolphins play reminded me of my friendship with Peg. When we were together, there was flow and harmony. We played well off each other's quirks and it was easy to laugh together. Every time we were together, it gave me a new perspective and a healing release. She just brought a Midwest balance to my life, and I was grateful.

♥ Love Beat

I wasn't just watching the dolphins playing in nature's playground, I was witnessing and absorbing their joyful energy. When I looked at the dolphin's smiling face, it was if he was holding a secret of life that he was going to tell me. It was as if Mother Nature herself was guiding me to her healing ocean waters and her dolphin angels held the secret rhythm that would keep me in the flow of forever love.

There was such harmony as the two mammals played together with such joy. They seemed to love each other and their connection flowed effortlessly. It was revealed to me the profound way they lived in oneness, in the pod and in the sea.

If I could only follow their lead, they're a perfect example of living in the higher frequencies of the love and joy. My heart became aware of the joy I was receiving, an infusion of healing from the dolphin's subliminal message.

I took a deep breath in and exhaled, "Aahhhhhhh." I took one more deep breath and exhaled out. I got slowly up off the rocks and the dolphins quickly moved away. I could see them rejoin the other pod of six further out in the ocean.

"They were there for me," I thought to myself and as I jumped off the last rock of the jetty. I could feel a surge of energy go down my legs that made me want to run.

During my jog, I flashed back to just a few days ago when David and I were running together on the beach. It brought me to a place when I felt my joy. I began to run faster and sea birds scattered when my feet splattered water on them.

I continued listening to my heart-pumping music to quiet the noise in my brain. I remembered what he told me when I asked him the question of running together. "He told me he likes to run side by side the best," I thought to myself.

It became so clear to me that I was running by myself far too long. I yearned for someone to run alongside me in life. I always wanted someone by my side, but I never slowed down long enough to run at someone else's pace. I was allowing myself the time to see how it feels with someone alongside me. It had me thinking about what my future would look like with David beside me.

I sat with the warm sun beating down on my face and the breeze gently blowing across my body to cool me. I listened to the rhythmic sounds of my feet firmly hitting the sand and I felt my heart in sync to its rhythm. When I got back to my beach chair, I immediately jotted down notes of my thoughts in my journal with one specific entry:

♥ Love Beat

I wrote in my journal: "I always run to clear my mind or I'm always running from something. Today I choose to run towards something, not chasing it but running to it. I choose to run into David's love. I am open to receive it."
7/18/2011

I also jotted down my lesson of the dolphin energy and how it would serve as one of the healing modalities to raise my frequency to love and joy. It brought me to the place of harmony. I was empowered, taking back the fragments of my heart through the moon, ocean, waves, dolphins and my dearest friends. It was then I realized my heart had begun its journey to oneness.

I was connecting to myself at a higher level and I wasn't afraid to trust in God, the Universe, Source or even David. I was in the state of heart-centered awareness and I allowed it to function instead of shutting it down like I did in the past. I had a shift in perspective and I was living in the state of present moment awareness. I no longer worried about time and all of its chains of restriction; I was flowing in the eternal Now.

For the rest of the trip, I couldn't help missing him, but I continued to laugh and enjoy my time with Peg. She was like family to me, it was important for me to connect with her more since this was our first trip, not to get her stamp of approval, but to give and receive love.

I valued her "get right to the point" truth about what she saw in the guy. I misjudged my boyfriends in the past, even when she met Mr. Fabulous, she could see something about him that I just couldn't see. She had a sharp eye for bullshit that I clearly missed.

I thought about my journey over the course of three weeks and how much it had changed from the beginning of the year. I was excited to see what could unfold in my life, in a new relationship, and in a new higher state of awareness for the truth. For the first time I didn't have a deadline, nor did I have to pray to survive, I could just be and let it happen in the time that it happens.

In my healing vortex of free moving emotions, I discovered the very thing I prayed about (having a man see my spirit) was actually happening to me. When I looked at David, I was envisioning his spirit, his essence, his frequency. I saw the energy of a pure heart.

It was so radiant to me, I could clearly see it didn't contain a trace of dark love in it. Instead it was filled with brilliant green and pink radiant light. It was safe and divine love combined. The brilliance of the light in his heart contained the Forever Love I had been searching for my whole life.

♥ Love Beat

You can see the heart of a person that you love if you just ask it to be revealed. The Universe will arrange ways to bring out the truth, but it is up to you to receive it. You must allow yourself the opportunity to embrace it as something that will serve its purpose to make your life better. If you see something negative in a person's heart you will need to address it right away. If it is not dealt with and hidden it will surface when least expected causing pain or rejection. All things work together for your good, so it doesn't matter when you see it, it must be addressed and it must be confronted.

I know that when I buried my father and old pattern relationships, my life began to get into harmony to what was declared at the beginning of the year. I was getting ready to receive my blessings, but I still didn't know it. I just felt things were changing. I embraced the change and I began to grow. I was in the summer of spiritual growth once again, but this time it was developing faster than I could keep up. Again, nature was my guide.

Peg and I arrived back in Raleigh at the end of the week and I immediately checked to see my schedule for the next few days. I had signed up for a weekend overnight shift to make up from all the traveling I had done. I had to be at work later that evening and the next night was my overnight shift.

I called David when we got close to my place. I knew I really missed him and hoped he missed me as much. I wondered if he would come see me or if I had to wait until Monday to be with him again.

"Hey, Peg is getting ready to drop me off at my place, but bad news I have to work at 8:00. Is that OK?"

"Yeah, I just want to see you. I don't care how long it's for!"

"Cool, we will be there in 5 minutes."

"OK, see you soon!"

It was a heartfelt reunion. I had more emotion when I saw him than I did before I left. He hopped out of his car and we hugged and kissed for a few minutes. He helped me lug my suitcase up the steps and told me he would take me to dinner before work.

He hung out with Jenny, while I took a shower and changed. David took me to take me to one of our cozy places next to the wine bar where we had our first date. We sat in a booth very excited to see each other just like little kids. I began telling him my antics with Peg. He laughed and told me he enjoyed hearing from me. I had so much love energy in my heart for him in that moment. I could feel he had it too.

"I think I'm going to write a book about love." I told him my desire to write a book after I came from my trip with Peg.

He looked at me and out popped the words, "I love you!"

My eyes opened wide and I said jokingly, "Ah. Oh…you said the 'L' word!"

He said it again, "I love you! You make me very happy and writing a book is a huge thing for you to share with me. I told you that you inspire me, you just didn't know how much."

My heart was beating so fast and it was full of love, I looked at him and said, "I love you too."

We enjoyed our dinner and when we walked to the car as we were leaving, he said, "I want to buy you some flowers. It's going to be a couple of days before we see each other again and I want you to look at them and be inspired."

The fact that he wanted to give me something visual to commemorate the moment, touched my heart. His thoughtfulness and his tender heart were attractive to me and I knew he cherished our time together. I was feeling wonderfully strange. I called it a calm delight.

He walked over to an outside flower vender and picked the most beautiful bouquet of orange gerbera daisies and other various flowers almost ready to bloom. I hopped in the car and he handed me the bouquet. I pushed my nose down in them, took a big whiff and smelled the fragrance of the flowers.

"These are very fragrant! They smell really nice!" I continued sniffing them.

"I think they have gardenias in there," he said when he took a quick survey of the bouquet.

We arrived at my apartment and I got out of his car with my flowers. We kissed good-bye and said, "I love you!"

"I love you, too."

I went up to put the flowers in water and to change into my black work pants.

My 8 p.m. to 11:30 p.m. shift zoomed by with my excitement over the "I love you" exchange, but when I came home around midnight, I found Jenny in the living room upset about her breakup with Jay.

She had been putting in so many hours on a grant project plus going to school, it made her vulnerability fair game for his frequent calls and texts. Even though Jay moved out of the apartment, he was still playing mind games with her and all her other circumstances were sucking the life out of her.

It was just a few short months ago that I was in my darkest energy state. I could read all the signs of her misery and could feel my compassion towards her.

I brewed a cup of herbal tea and sat down to help coach her through her break up blues. I also brought her up to date with my relationship with David.

The next morning we both got up with a new perspective and plenty of rest. I wanted to run in the woods on my favorite path. I had just returned from the beach and went straight into work. I discovered my three weeks of nature wisdom worked the best when I was in it. I needed another nature fix to keep me from sabotaging my new relationship.

In reflecting back, I had discovered so many of my failed relationships had been a product of my own self-sabotaging fears and dark love; I didn't want to fall into the same trap. I glanced at the flowers he gave me sitting on my dresser. When I did, I noticed the most brilliant colors I had ever seen. The flowers had bloomed into a spectacular array of colors and fragrances. I bent over to take a good whiff; it was like a magical potion.

I turned my iPod on and put my ear buds in and began the journey in the woods. I dialed up my favorite song by Dirty Vegas and sang out loud "…as I start a brand new day, my life will never be the same!"

Running on the path was different than running on the beach. When I heard the roar of the ocean, my revelations spoke to my heart loud and clear, but on the path in the woods the insight whispers where more subtle and symbolic. I saw a patch of wild flowers blooming on the bank near the creek and I flashed to the image of the beautiful flowers that were sitting on my dresser. I thought about David and instantly smiled.

♥ *Love Beat*

My thought was, "David is good for me." Then I received the biggest revelation I had ever had about picking out the right men. My inner wisdom revealed, "I was ALWAYS good for the guy but the guy wasn't good for me!" This was an eye-opening experience since in most relationships I had, I would hear things like, "You are too good for me" or "I don't deserve you." Those are men code phrases for the truth of who they are. When you hear those phrases it means that it's true. You are too good for them. You are living in a higher vibration!

But beware you are about to be dumped or cheated on because of the hidden dark love energy still dwelling inside of them. It is a form of manipulation to make you feel as if you need to try harder, living in the energy of struggle. Relationships are work but they are not struggle or worry.

Then I thought about it again, "Oh my God! I always prayed to make me a good thing and I was!"

"I was good for the guy, but he wasn't good for me."

"David is good for me." I said it, over and over, "David is good for me!"

I discovered I was getting exactly what I prayed for, for me to be a good thing but I wasn't in harmony with the vibration of forever love. I needed to add that the man has to be good for me too!

For whatever reason, (old pattern thinking) I always thought it was my responsibility to do the inner work to be a better person, but it is also the choice of the other person who has to want change too. They also need to want to do the inner work and be clear on their desires. It is better for you to already know the changes you have made and the changes in the man. How do we do this? You will know them by their fruits.

A biblical principal that means whatever is inside a person will always come out of a person. If he has a bad temper, he is always going to have a bad temper, unless he recognizes it as something that isn't the best version of him and wants the behavior to change. With Divine inner guidance and self-discipline, he will not have a bad temper, no matter what happens to him. He will get angry and that is okay, because anger is an emotion, but he will not be abusive, belittling or physically violent.

The fruit will appear as a heated discussion with passionate views, no judgment if you don't agree and a simple solution to keep peace or reveal a different point of view.

♥ Love Beat

In all of my relationships I spent most of my time compromising to their way of thinking and losing bits of myself to be accepted by that person. Simply put, we may be good for them but the love energy that they are giving back may not be good for us. It could be the only love energy they know. You have the power. It is up to you to decide if a man is or isn't good for you.

If you recognize he isn't good for you and you ignore it, be prepared for some not so pleasant moments and painful emotional situations. You will need to eventually clear the negative energy from the relationship and mop up those hurts before the cycle of energy draws more of the same to you.

The flowers brought me a vibrant moment of clarity and I could see we were both good for each other and our energy together flowed in harmony. I could feel the electricity of all the possibilities.

I turned a corner on the trail and saw a deer grazing near my running path. Normally when I saw one, I would jingle my keys to have the deer dash into the woods for safety. This time I slowed down and walked past the deer in slow motion.

I stopped to look at her and she stood very still and very beautiful. She watched me with her nose twitching, but didn't move. Ever so slowly, I continued to walk past her along the path and she bent down to start grazing. I was no threat to her and she was an exquisite beauty to watch.

Suddenly I saw her ears perk straight up and her head shot up tall and straight. I heard the voices of two ladies approaching us on the same part of the trail. The deer twitched her nose and tail and scampered into the woods. I picked up my pace and continued running.

♥ Love Beat

My deer encounter of the first kind was a lesson about fear. I was prepared to see the deer on the path but never stopped to really "see" it. I saw it as a threat, something that was going to hurt me if I approached her territory. I was afraid of the deer, so I made a noise to scare it off. By making noise, my vibration became higher than the deer's and the tables were turned. The deer was afraid of me and ran.

This time I slowed my rhythm to the deer's peaceful state. I stayed in its stillness and saw the beauty of the deer. I was able to breathe the same air and enjoy the surroundings as much as the animal. I was grounded and peaceful watching the beauty of nature unfold in front of me.

My question to myself was, "How many times do we run from beautiful moments in our lives because we are afraid?" If I could overcome my fear of the deer and experience all its beauty, I was also free to overcome my fear of trusting men and allow my love to unfold with David.

I reminded myself of all the negative fearful emotions I released on the beach and how the dolphins showed me harmony. For the first time, I viewed the beauty of David's forever love. I was finally open to receive the love I had been searching for my whole life and all I had to do was believe.

I came back to my room and the flowers were even more spectacular than when I had left. I snapped a picture of them and sent the image to David with a caption that read," "Thank you! Look at them! They are simply wonderful!"

He thanked me for sharing the picture and enjoyed the fact the flowers made me happy. The flowers represented the beauty of forever love and how my love was in full bloom.

I had been giving my mom details of my new relationship with David each week and I also shared my revelations about love. She was my biggest cheerleader and would always tell me she felt good about him. Maybe she could sense my happiness or she just knew it was time, but she told me she recognized the energy of peace in my voice.

Only a few weeks after we said our "I love you's," David whisked me off to his father's timeshare in the mountains of Boone County, North Carolina. Boone was known for its beautiful quaint mountain towns and good wines.

David's father had been going up there for many years and David wanted me to share the experience. He had planned for us to go to Grandfather Mountain first.

The road going up to the mountain was winding and steep. We crept along the road where tourists stopped to take pictures of the vistas at lookout points.

I was giddy like a little girl and couldn't wait to get to the top; we parked at a lookout point and got out of the car. Fog was covering most of the vistas, but it was still lush and green. We walked towards a suspended bridge over a gorge.

"I can't look down," I informed him.

"Yeah it's sort of scary. You will be fine!" He guided me to more solid footing.

"Look over on this side." He showed me a mound of rocks and helped me plant my feet on the secure platform.

"Wow!" I looked all around I was in the moment with no fear. Suddenly, a swoosh of wind blew by my face. It was cool and moist and invigorating. It was a cloud!

"I breathed a cloud! I breathed a cloud!" I said with glee.

"Yes, I guess we did! That's pretty cool, I would have never thought of it like that!" he said sounding amazed.

"I have to get a pin!" I exclaimed.

That was my new habit ever since I went to Ocracoke. Everywhere I traveled, I bought a pin representing the adventure and put them on my cowboy hat. My enthusiasm was contagious; David took me to the souvenir gift shop at the top of the mountain. I bought two pins, one for Grandfather Mountain where I breathed the cloud and one that looked like a license plate that read: "RIDE – share the journey."

Our trip to the mountains solidified my feelings towards David. I had opened my heart to receive love and was not afraid. I allowed his love to inspire me and I lived in each moment. He was kind and protective of my heart. I knew he would be the one who could cherish it in a way that I needed. I found my authentic self and he loved me for it. I didn't have to hide or mask who I was to please him.

Each day I spent with him was a day that I had more respect for his quiet strength and integrity. I observed him accepting my friends wholeheartedly with no judgment and his spiritual side was deep and pure.

While we were on the mountain, I was sitting on our deck appreciating nature, looking at the mountaintops and breathing the crisp mountain air, when my heart whispered a poem.

💜 *Love Beat*

"Just Breathe"

The air I breathe is you.

You are the reason I breathe so freely,

You are the reason I breathe life.

You are the reason I breathe peace.

You are the wind of hope that propels me to my destiny.

You are the long relaxing breeze of the ocean that refreshes me.

You are the exhilarating cloud in the mountain that excites me.

You are the one in whom I would draw my last breath with...you are my muse and inspiration.

You make me breathe.

I instinctively felt a future with him. He was the refuge for my restless soul he was like the Eagle's song, "Peaceful Easy Feeling!"

David and I spent the rest of our summer together continuing to grow stronger in our love. I kept up with my calls to my mom and she was always upbeat about her health and excited to hear about my relationship.

I had no drama with David like in the past. His daughters loved me and I got along with his family. We were always laughing and in perfect harmony. It seemed as if everything was in alignment and balance in my life.

CHAPTER 9

Going Home

It was close to Labor Day weekend, when I received a phone call from my younger sister, Shelly. "Laurie, we have bad news. We just got back from the doctor's office and mom's cancer came back. We have a doctor's appointment next week to discuss the options, but mom is not feeling well right now."

"Oh no! Do you think I should come up? Is it that bad?" My heart began racing. "Oh no, not my mom," I thought to myself. I was just coming to terms with the loss of my father.

"Let's see what the doctor says and we will take it from there." She reassured me that my mom would call me after a nap, but ever since they came from the appointment her energy was drained. I hung up the phone and sat with a blank look on my face.

David asked, "What's wrong, babe?"

I stared at the wall and then looked at him, "My mom's cancer came back." He could see the tears well up in my eyes. He came over to the couch where I was sitting and just hugged me. It was a warm, sincere loving hug and I never wanted to let him go.

The next day Shelly called back and said, "I took mom to the hospital."

"What? What happened?" I was shocked.

"Mom wasn't eating and her ankles were swelling up. I didn't like what I was seeing, so I did some Internet searches and thought it may be blood clots. It turned out that I was right and she is being treated with blood clotting medicine in the hospital. They will be monitoring her and she will be there for a few days. I thought you would like to know."

"Of course! Thanks for telling me. Did you call Bobby and Frankie yet?" I was getting anxious about what to do next.

"Yeah, I left them messages to call, but I also let them know mom was in the hospital. I will be hearing from them and I'll give them the details."

"Well, Shell, I am coming up now. I will call you later when I get my tickets and figure out work issues."

There was no way I was going to be left out. I had to be with my family in such a crisis. When my dad passed, Shelly was protective of mom and she kept me at arm's length. She always seemed to think she had to handle my parent's health situations by herself. I sensed I was needed and wanted to be by my mother's side. No one was going to stop me from being there.

David was in another room and couldn't see me pacing the floor or hear the anxiety in my voice. When I went into the same room with him, I let him know my mom was in the hospital and in a few minutes we were booking a flight to St. Louis. I planned on staying a few weeks.

♥ Love Beat

It had been less than three months in our relationship, when it dawned on me that we knew each other pretty well. David had compassion in my moment of crisis and was willing to do whatever it took to help me navigate through the troubled time. Compassion comes as a fruit of feeling all energies of fear, joy, pain, sadness and anger but it is detached of absorbing those emotions for themselves. With compassion you are able to give a person what they need in order to direct the energy toward movement or change because you can recognize what they are feeling.

He jumped into the role of assisting. He was there to assist me with his support, emotionally and financially, and he was able to calm my panic and make logical suggestions. He was always giving me peaceful loving energy in the midst of my emotional storm. He was a grounding source and we were able to make rational decisions together instead of the turmoil I went through with other men.

I was so grateful for David. He was the total opposite of Mr. Fabulous. When I was going through my father's passing, Mr. Fabulous could barely squeeze out a tear and practically told me to suck it up and move on! His indifference put me through agony and I thought about the years I wasted with him and all his family drama.

I remembered, at 50 years old, I was of just waiting. I wanted to be in a relationship, no matter what I had to endure. I believed that time was running out for me. I thought he was my last chance at love but I was wrong and I allowed the fear of time have power over most of my decisions during that time in my life.

Fear of Time was now roaring back at me like a lion, "You don't have enough time with your mother." Instead of fearing it, I was going to confront it. I wouldn't be facing my fear alone; David was right by my side. I changed my view of how I would spend time with my mother and enjoy each moment with her.

Then it dawned on me, I was never alone in this journey. I was a co-creator with God and the Universe. I had set a declaration over my life at the beginning of the year and entered a season of manifestation. I recognized in order to get through this uncertain period of time I would need support and trust. I needed to have this journey with David. I knew with him, I was able to trust in his safe love and for him to hold me close when I was fearful. Fear and love were separate and I recognized the difference.

When I arrived at the hospital early that evening, her television was on but her eyes were closed. "Mom? I'm here."

She cracked her eyes open and smiled as I walked closer to her bed. "Hi, honey!" eyes opened wide and she reached for my hand. I leaned over to give her a hug and kissed her cheek.

"How are you feeling?" I asked.

"I'm OK. The swelling in my ankles just started a few days ago. I thought it was an after-effect from the chemo. I'm glad Shelly was there to take me to the hospital," she explained.

"Me too mom. Me too. I am going to be staying here with you for a little while, OK?

She asked, "Do you mean here at the hospital or at the house?"

"Both, I want to help you and give the family some regroup time," I replied.

I could see the excitement in her face build, "That's wonderful and you are my angel. That chair folds out into a bed and Frankie comes to see me when he gets off of work somewhere around 2 a.m."

I could tell in her eyes that she needed us to rally around her. She really didn't like hospitals, doctors or nurses. She was a good patient, but she didn't want to be in a position to need them. She was a strong woman of God and used her faith and scriptures to believe in miracles. I believed that also, but at some point I had to convince my mother (and myself) that God uses doctors, as well as many other holistic ways to heal too.

Mom began to liven up and wanted to know the details of my relationship with David. She acted like a reporter for the *National Inquirer* asking every juicy question for every juicy answer! I showed her a video message from him that he recorded on my cell phone at the airport and she smiled and said, "He seems real nice and that accent!"

"Yeah I know! It's a thick one isn't it?" We laughed but then I got serious, "Mom, what is happening with your health?" I wanted to hear her response and look in her eyes.

She said, "We will be talking to the doctor tomorrow when everyone is here. I don't know what else to tell you, it all happened so quickly. I have other things to talk to you about, about the family." She seemed anxious and wanted to get something off her chest. That is when I entered into the war zone. It was the battlefield of cancer, filled with family feuds and emotional land mines.

She informed me, in addition to coping with her diagnosis, each of my siblings was going through a difficult time of their own.

Bobby's wife had passed away earlier that year and he was trying to cope. My sister was burnt out (from being the caretaker) and having health issues of her own, and Frankie had marital issues and moved out of his house. It was an explosion of emotional proportions.

My mother told me that she was caught up in the middle of it all. She had been spending hours counseling each of us, trying to cope with the loss of my father and trying to forget about her own cancer battle. It was wearing her down.

Apparently when she was counseling my sister-in-law about my brother's indiscretions, something in her heart was triggered that she had buried deep inside of her. She had told me that my father was unfaithful; she was devastated but forgave him. I had no idea how to handle the information. I thought she might be doped up from the drugs, because I only saw a devoted husband my entire life.

I didn't understand the reasoning behind her telling me this, except that she wanted to unburden herself. I listened to her as she shared her feelings. I held her hand and shed a few tears. For some reason I was holding all my emotions inside of me.

"Mommy, I'm so sorry you carried this your whole life. I can understand why you are so upset with everyone." I felt as if she was handing me the torch to continue to counsel the family because of my life-coach training (even when I was still trying to coach myself). In her mind, I was the oldest and the "big sister" and it was my new assignment to keep the family drama at a minimum. It was comforting for her to know that I would be talking to each of my siblings and hopefully giving them wisdom in their situations. She may have been relieved from the task, but I didn't know if they would listen to me. I was considered the "outsider" ever since I moved to Florida the first time.

After a couple of hours of catch up time with mom, the nurse gave her the last dose of her meds for the night and she fell asleep. I sat and pondered all the information she disclosed, only to find myself unsettled and restless. I was strategizing ways to have some alone time to talk with each of my brothers and sister. I sent a text to David to let him know I made it there safely and how much I missed him.

I looked over at my mom sleeping, she looked peaceful. I wondered how much time I had left with her and if she would ever meet David. I picked up my journal and wrote down the day's events and finally fell asleep.

At 2 a.m., my brother Frankie came to the room to see mom. We stepped out in the hall and hugged. I was happy to see him, but sad to hear the news of his broken marriage. We made a date to talk and have lunch and went back into the room where he sat on the foot of mom's bed. He gently rubbed her shin and said, "Mama, I'm here."

Her face lit up. Frankie was always the one who made her smile the biggest. He was her golden child after her two miscarriages. How could I tell him that his marital situation broke her heart and triggered something else that broke her heart so long ago? I just didn't know how to handle it and I fell asleep thinking about it.

The next morning, I was somewhat rested but anxious to hear the doctor's report and the next steps in her treatment. It wasn't good news. The cancer came back as a more aggressive version and had already spread to her stomach. The only hope was to get in a clinical trial for a new drug that shrinks that type of cancer. We all sat around her hospital room discussing options and outcomes. The bottom line was the doctor's options would only possibly slow down the cancer, with a less than 50/50 chance it would work. My mother needed us to believe in a miracle.

After the consultation mom wanted to rest, I stepped out of her room and into a lounge area to call David.

"Hi honey, I'm calling to let you know that my mom's condition has gotten worse. She will be in the hospital a couple more days and I will be staying with her. They are monitoring the blood clots and she will be able to go home if the meds work by then. I will keep you posted but I gotta go, I hear her calling me!"

"OK, tell your mom I am praying for her and I love you! Call me later. Things are fine here with me," he said sweetly.

It was later that afternoon when the visitors began to arrive. My sister and her husband came back to sit with mom while I went to the cafeteria. The reality of my mother's condition was hard for me to comprehend. She was doing so well throughout the spring and summer months. I couldn't wrap my mind around the prospect of losing her.

My upbeat love tempo with David had now slowed down to a snail's pace. I found myself trying to take care of the remnants of my family. After three days in the hospital with my mom, I was able to bring her home by the end of the first week of my stay. I called everyone to let them know she was home.

"Let me get you in first and then I will get your things, OK? Mom, I am here to help take care of you, please let me." I gathered her things and she was very slow walking into the house.

She wasn't my mother anymore. Instead of a spry, animated person, she was weak and fragile from the hospital stay and the news of the cancer spreading. It took all of her energy to walk down the hall to her bedroom. She was trying to keep a strong face and show me that she was still strong, but I could tell she was giving up the fight. I lay down next to her and cuddled. I was there for a few minutes and I asked, "Do you want the TV on?"

"No, that's OK, I think I will rest for a while."

I got up and closed the door behind me, sat in the living room and stared at the walls. This was the house where I grew up and heard my dad's conga music playing and my mother laughing. It is where I learned to dance in life and to have joy. It was no longer the same place. The music stopped and it was quiet, so very quiet.

I pulled out some of the pamphlets from the hospital about nutrition and began to read them. I was interrupted by a phone call from my brother Frankie asking to fix our favorite meal for a Sunday family dinner. I thought it was a great idea to have everyone over to welcome mom home. The next few days were rough and my mother seemed to be getting worse. She was barely eating. She had some moments of being strong, funny and capable, but there were more times she didn't have the strength and rested often.

By late Sunday afternoon, my brothers came to the house and fixed dinner while mom stayed in bed. While we were in the kitchen visiting, I was able to tell them about my new relationship with David. During our conversation my sister called to tell us she wasn't able to join us, due to a previous church commitment. My brothers couldn't believe that she would have passed on a family event as sick as mom was and we began to speculate on her detached behavior.

An hour passed and mom finally came out of her room; she had dressed herself and put on a big smile. She told us that she wasn't hungry enough to eat, but to go ahead without her. She visited with us for about an hour and trudged back into her bedroom. I followed her and made sure she was comfortable. When I returned to the kitchen Bobby asked, "How long has she been like that?"

"Ever since we came back from the hospital," I replied.

"It's not good that she's isn't eating," he said.

"I know, I have been giving her the nutritional drinks and she eats some oatmeal in the morning. She likes apples and snacks on them during the day." We all couldn't get over how quickly she deteriorated. While she was sleeping we talked about how we were going to handle the circumstances after the doctor's consultation and her blood plasma transfusion.

I had a hard time sleeping that night; the realization of losing her had me so restless, I couldn't turn off my brain. When I finally did fall asleep I had a dream that I believe prepared me for the next several days.

In my dream my mother was in her mid-thirties (she was still sick but younger). The family was on a ship in the middle of the ocean and we were talking and laughing together. The next thing that happened was that my mother jumped off the ship. I saw her halfway through the water as she plunged into the deep blue sea. I saw a pod of dolphins swirling around her, but they never surfaced. She disappeared and I couldn't see the dolphins anymore, all I could see were the bubbles. I began crying because the feeling of loss came upon me. When the last bubble dissipated, a dolphin came up to the surface of the water and smiled at me. It was at that moment, I knew my mother was gone. When I looked at the dolphin's eye in my dream, a healing energy was released and I had intuition imparted on me that the end was near.

♥ Love Beat

Since making the decision to open my heart to love's energy, I was more in tune with everything that surrounded me. I saw everything as energy and I would be able to navigate by my intuition. I was building trust in myself and trust in others. The dream with the dolphin gave me an insight that my mother didn't have much time, but there was also a healing property in the dolphin's eyes when he looked at me. His smiling face was full of joy, like he knew a secret. It was the same look that I saw earlier in the summer when I was at the beach with Peggy. Again, it was a symbol of going with the flow, the dolphin was telling me that my mother was in a peaceful state of flow and she was slowly transitioning to leave this earth.

That morning, I woke up crying. It took me a little while to shake off the feeling left by the dream and get my mother ready to go to the oncologist. My sister and I sat with her during her blood transfusion and it seemed to give her a bit more energy.

We wheeled her into the conference room of the oncologist, where my brothers were already sitting waiting for her to arrive. We all sat at the around the table and heard these words, "There is nothing more we can do here. It's too late for a clinical trial and there is not enough of the drug to go around for this type of aggressive cancer. It is now time to get Hospice involved."

I will never forget the expression on her face. It was resolve. It was clear to her that she was going to die. On the way home she just stared out the window and thanked me for being here for her. I turned into the driveway and she said, "I've lived a good life. I have four beautiful children who love the Lord. What else can I ask for?"

I said, "More time. You can ask for more time, Mom." She didn't say anything and I took it as a cue that she had given up fighting. I didn't react to her non-response and helped her out of the car. The next couple of days, we had nurses come to the house to check her vitals, give her medication and to help us with Hospice options.

Shelly and I were beginning to stress out about caring for her. I knew I was not capable of being a caretaker and Shelly had been taking care of her since my father passed away. We both discussed the best options for us and told our brothers about the decision we made to bring her to a facility if there were beds available.

I was a total wreck from lack of sleep and emotionally drained. My trip was booked for two weeks and I was scheduled to attend Peg's younger daughter's wedding when I returned. I planned on going and felt a real need to step away from St. Louis to regroup and reclaim my emotional sanity. I missed David terribly and I needed to see him. He was the only joy in my aching heart.

By the end of the week, we moved mom into the Hospice facility and later that day I left for Raleigh. It was heart wrenching but I also knew it was the right thing to do. On the plane, I began to sort out some of my feelings from the past two weeks. The sense of loss made me feel alone, not just as a child losing both parents, but also as a woman. I could barely think of my mother so frail and weak. She had always been my rock, the glue to our family and my source of strength my whole life.

I felt no guilt in leaving the situation for a couple of days, I knew that in order to live my life, I would have to let go of hers. I couldn't stay in the middle of my broken family's drama and wrap my mind around the circumstances that had taken place, the infidelity, betrayal, death and joy. The trip home had the makings of a Lifetime movie!

In Raleigh, I called my mother three times the next day. She was upbeat and happy at the facility. There was a piano there and Shelly played music for her twice a day. My mother's concerns were comforted by the 24/7 care she received. The whole time I had stayed with her, she told me she didn't want to be a burden to the family and I tried to convince her that she wasn't. I was just not equipped to handle her health needs and she couldn't tell me what she needed. It was frustrating not knowing how to help her.

Back in Raleigh, I felt like I had a split personality. I went to the wedding with David with waves of emotion hitting me like a tidal wave at any given moment. Peg was happy to see me and concerned about my mental state, but her concern was short-lived. As the mother of the bride, she was too busy to focus on me. Her husband Dave was a proud father and the wedding was beautiful. When we arrived at the reception, I just wanted to dance!

Every song that came on, I pulled David on the dance floor. We danced song after song until a wave of emotion crept into my mind and then I would run out into the hallway and cry. I kept thinking about the song, "Turn, Turn, Turn," and how there is a time to laugh and a time to cry. I was living both at the same time.

The next day David and I talked in great detail about my mother's condition. I sensed the end was near and wanted to get back to St. Louis as soon as possible. We made the decision to drive back and stay for as long as it took to be with her during her last days. I was hoping that she would hang in there to meet David. We loaded up his SUV with our suitcases (and Monty) early Monday morning and began the drive to St. Louis, from Raleigh, NC.

On our trip through the Tennessee Mountains my sister called. "Laurie, I just got a call from the nurse and she told me that mom is getting worse. She said that she thinks it will be sometime this week. Are you coming back?"

I said, "Yes, David is with me and we are driving now. You tell her I am coming! Make sure you tell her!"

"Of course, I know she will fight. The nurse says it will be a couple of days at least. Frankie is flying Aunt Vivian in from Texas to be with her, too. I will keep you posted as the day goes on."

"OK, we will make it in time. I know it!" I was positive and when I hung up the phone I told David that she took a turn for the worse. We drove straight through, only stopping for gas. I was on a mission. I wanted my mother to meet David and he wanted that too.

♥ *Love Beat*

It was the intention of both of us that caused her spirit to fight. I knew she wanted to meet him. We both wanted to see her and with the "power of us" in agreement, it aligned us with perfect timing. I wasn't anxious about making it in time. I was now in harmony with the Universe and God's plan. I had a peace in my heart that we would be there at the best possible time. I had peace in my heart that we were going to be safe and she was going to meet him face to face.

The sun was setting over the Mississippi River, when we drove across the bridge to St. Louis. I called to get an update on her condition and to let her know we were almost there. My mother was sitting up and alert. Her sister had just arrived and bolstered her spirits.

Everyone was in her room when we walked in. She looked pale, but still had a sparkle in her eyes. Everyone left the room to give David and me a chance to talk with her privately. She smiled and I sat next to her on the bed. "Mom, this is David."

He took her fragile hand said, "Nice to meet you, Sarah. I want to tell you that I love your daughter very much!"

I looked at her face and she was still smiling. She took my hand and squeezed it and said, "He's nice!" It was if she was giving me her blessing and she said under her breath, "Thank you, Lord." I walked out of the room to let David talk to her and to find out her condition from the nurses.

David had a short conversation with her and told her how much he loved me and wanted a future with me. I know that made her happy to hear him express his intentions. I was delighted to hear him tell her how real our love was.

After all the visitors, my mom was coming in and out of awareness due to the pain medication. She was happy to see all the family and especially happy to see her sister. David and I were so tired from the 16-hour drive, so we drove to my parents' house to unload our car and to put Monty somewhere safe, where he could eat and sleep. I planned on going back later to bring her some of the things she asked for.

David took time to meet other members of my family. They fell in love with his eagerness to be of help in all the chaos. While we were discussing our next steps as a family, David went to the grocery store and bought food for family that were staying at the house. He was so compassionate, as he consoled each of my family members. I flashed back to the time when I was with Mr. Fabulous and how he couldn't be bothered by my feelings during my dad's passing. It was wrong of me to even compare the two, but David's sincere concern for each of us made me love him even more.

That evening, I drove by myself to visit mom. She was resting and woke up as soon as I arrived. I had slipped a vitamin C facial capsule into the front pocket of my jeans and pulled it out.

"Are you awake, mommy?" I asked

"Yes, Sweetheart. I'm awake." She was weak and her voice was shaky.

"I brought some 'slappy' for your face," I said. (Slappy is what we called the cosmetic products she bought on the shopping networks, because sellers would frantically slap the women around when they put product on their faces.)

"Which one did you bring?" She asked and I could tell it bolstered her spirit.

"I got the vitamin C capsule," I replied.

"Oh good, put it on me please. My skin feels so dry."

I broke the capsule and dabbed the liquid gel onto on my fingertips. I gently rubbed the serum on her cheeks and her forehead. She smiled with delight and she looked peaceful and serene.

"I love you, mommy. You are my mommy and I love you forever."

"I love you too, honey. You are my first baby."

"Mom, I'm going to be alright. You know that, don't you?" I leaned over to get closer and buried my face in her shoulder. She took her other arm and laid her hand on my back. I could feel her spirit fighting, yet her body so weak.

"Your David is a real gentleman. He is good for you."

I pulled my head off her shoulder and said, "Yes mom, he is good for me and I am good for him. I love him very much. We are going to be OK. He loves me too. I'm so happy you got to meet him."

"He has a kind heart." She took my hand and squeezed it hard and said, "I think I need to sleep now." She was in between states I think, but was still fighting.

"We will come back in the morning, OK?"

"Yes, OK. Everyone will come?"

"Yes mom, everyone is coming at different times. Shelly and Mike, Vivian, David and I are all coming after we eat breakfast."

"Oh good, see you tomorrow. Good night."

I kissed her on the forehead, pulled up her crocheted blanket and closed the door behind me. I could feel the tears coming from my eyes. I was still in shock when I walked to the car. My mother was dying and there was nothing I could do about it. I drove home and let the tears flow because I wasn't strong enough to let her go.

♥ Love Beat

Instinctively, I knew my mother didn't have much time, but I also knew she was at peace. It was a blessing to have her meet David, since most of my life she prayed for me to meet my soul mate. I could tell that she felt complete by meeting him and was truly happy for me. Deep down inside of her, I think she knew I finally found forever love.

The next morning I woke up to the smell of bacon and coffee. David had gotten up early and started to make breakfast for us. I saw a side of his personality that was nurturing and kind. He was giving of himself so selflessly; it was a quality I saw inside of him but had not really seen on display. He was a man of word and deed, which impressed me most of all. The house began to stir as people started waking up. One by one, we headed towards the kitchen like zombies gravitating to the coffee maker. Each of us poured a cup and sat down at the kitchen table.

"Vivian, how do you like your eggs cooked?" David asked in a pleasant tone.

"Oh, thank you, David, but I will just have a piece of toast this morning," she replied.

"I like mine scrambled, honey," I said and Shelly chimed in, "Me too!"

Mike was walking into the kitchen rubbing his eyes, "I smell bacon!" We laughed and he joined us. After breakfast, we all got ready to head up to the Hospice House together, (until Shelly and Mike opted to go later that morning so they could check on their dogs). David, my aunt Viv and I were heading to her room when we saw my two brothers entering the doorway of mom's room. They had just arrived and I wanted to give them time alone with her. We waited a few minutes and entered the room. Everyone was gathered around her bedside, she was alert and funny.

My brother Frankie knelt down by her side and whispered something to her and she whispered back. He stood up and said, "I got it! I got the secret of Grandma Jewels! And how to make them just like hers! It's the thimble!"

Grandma Jewels were Christmas cookies mom made ever since Frankie was two years old. He would help her make the cookies and wanted to take over the tradition someday. Mom would slowly reveal her secret recipes to him over the years. He had to find out the last secret ingredient to make his taste like hers and she finally told him. It was as if he hit the lottery.

I cornered my brother Bob in the hallway and asked how he was doing. He said," This has been a rough year for me, first Sue (his wife) and now mom."

"I know," and gave him a big hug.

We were in the middle of our clench when Shelly and Mike rushed into the facility, "How's mom?"

"She's good, she is talking with Frankie and Aunt Viv is in there with her. I was just giving them some time together."

"Oh, the nurse called and said she was getting worse," Shelly explained.

"Well, when I saw her she was smiling, alert and happy. I guess we should go check it out." It was if she knew we were all there. She was getting weaker and her face grimaced with pain at times. "I can't watch my mother die," I said to David and he held me tight.

Frankie walked out of the room with tears in his eyes. "I can't watch this," he said.

"I just said that to David! I can't watch my mother die. She is life to me!" I could hear music coming from her room now, Shelly had brought her CD player and put in her CD and began to sing to mom. A sweet presence of energy and light began to fill the room. My aunt began to pray out loud. I felt as if right on cue, Shelly sensed the time was near and began to usher in the peace of God by singing and giving praise. It was a sweet song of joy and peace that filled her room and the halls. After a while, I peeked in the room and saw my mother's eyes open and she was smiling. I watched her, as her eyes were glistening and bright, but her body so frail.

Shelly left the music on as David and I walked into the room. David told her once again how much he loved me and then I asked him for a minute alone with her.

"Mom. I told you last night, I will be OK. I am fine and now it is alright for you to meet Jesus. Everyone will be OK… it's OK to go be with Jesus. Goodbye, mommy. I love you!" I kissed her face and left the room. I wiped the tears from my eyes. I said goodbye to my mother.

In my mind, I could understand she was dying, but in my heart she was still very much alive. I could hear her little voice telling me funny things, making up funny words, giving me godly wisdom and plain common sense. She gave me life in the natural world, but gave so much more to my spiritual life. To me she will be an eternal being guiding me through my life. Only a few short hours later, my mother left this earth; she died peacefully and with dignity. Each one of us had our last words of love and individual moments with her.

♥ Love Beat

No one ever knew my mother's pain. She wasn't the type of woman who poured her problems on anyone. She went to the throne instead of the phone and she was full of faith. Even in the end, she revealed to me her disappointment and misery but she was never afraid to die. When I asked if she wanted more time, she never answered me and at that point I knew she was ready to go. I believe her life was too difficult and painful without my father around (she had known him since she was a teen). They were the kind of couple who were the best when they were together and not apart.

CHAPTER 10

A New Rhythm

After we left mom's hospital room, it was 6:30 p.m. We walked to a restaurant next door to grab a bite. Frankie went home to get ready for his show that evening. At 7:05 p.m., we received the phone call that mom had passed. It was then I realized I didn't have a normal relationship when it came to my parents. I detached from them physically, long ago when I moved to Florida.

Since I wasn't around them physically, my spiritual and soul connection to them was very strong. I wasn't in the fray of family emotional drama, I was outside of it and would get the best parts of them. We talked about heart matters and laughed about goofy things that happened at work. I know in my lowest points I wore them down with my tears, but they would still be proud of me as I navigated my way through life single-handedly. I chose to step away from the family bullshit and I kept my distance and my peace.

♥ *Love Beat*

The prompting for self-discovery led me away from my parents. I needed to move away from them in order to mature. I carried with me the pain of rejection when my father compared me to his entertainer mother and never told me I was pretty. The emotional baggage he carried from his own rejection infiltrated my life and the lack of support from him pushed me away. By doing that, I found myself attaching myself to men who were wrong for me and I lived under the cloud of struggle. I was finally able to break free of living in that low energy vibration. I was picking up the broken fragments of my heart into a place of wholeness.

The inner growth cause me to work through negative emotions towards my father. During my "God Years," Divine love made it possible to forgive him; understanding that he was doing the best he could do at the time.

I was finally able to bury the most recent negative emotions, as the memories surfaced during the conga ritual of release. I realized I had carried old hurts from the past (most of my life) and had to energetically release them into the ocean and transmute them back into Divine love.

Even though my love for my father was cloudy at times, my love for my mother was far less complicated. We had a safe love with only a dose of judgment, especially when it came to the men in my life. She was always there to give me spiritual advice and to encourage me to keep my faith, especially when it looked bleak. She would always pray for me and I would feel alive once again. My mother kept my faith alive by resuscitating my belief in God and encouraging me to believe that all things were possible.

There was such a joy in my heart introducing her to David. I could tell she approved of him and blessed our relationship, which gave me great peace. I know she was thinking he was an answered prayer.

In many ways when my mother died, I felt closer to her. She had been "life" to me and I couldn't think of her as dead. She gave birth to me, a physical life, but she also was my spiritual teacher and guide. Instead of grieving for her and carrying the burden of sorrow in my heart, I decided to breath in more of her wonderful spirit, release my attachments and let her go. It was a very difficult way to think and harder to do.

♥ *Love Beat*

I knew I had to feel the grief, but I also had to let go of all my emotional attachments to her, especially any buried negative ones. If I lived my life in the lower energy of grief, those energies would feed other lower energies and depression or apathy would be knocking at the door. I chose to laugh instead of cry.

Since my New Year's declaration and my conga release ritual, my life had transformed into living in a higher energy of Divine love. The higher love frequency helped me embrace my mother's safe love, her spirit and even her death. I knew that at some point, if I carried the energy of sadness around with me (which was caused by loss), I would go back into the "struggling" state of being.

I knew my mother was a joyful person and she wouldn't want me crying and unhappy because she was gone. I embraced her time on this earth and the time I had to spend with her until the end. I embraced my love for her by celebrating her life. We all did.

After dinner we all went to the house to sort out details of the Hospice paperwork and discuss her memorial service. It all happened so fast we barely had any time to get her affairs in order. The house was empty. All that was left were decades of memories on the walls of the house where we grew up. I heard no conga music. There were no twirls. The music had stopped. It was quiet and still.

We moved the coffee table and sofa to clear a space on the living room floor and dumped out a big suitcase of pictures they had been saved with all our memories. We each grabbed a manila envelope and started picking out our favorite photos. We circled around a pile of pictures in the middle of the floor and gathered old photos of my mom to use in the memorial service.

It was too emotionally draining for my brother Frankie to do a show, just hours after the passing of my mom. He left his gig during the first break and joined us at the house to help him process his emotions. He started shuffling the photos around and for the first time, I saw his spirit beaten down. He was usually a high-energy person, but he absorbed the heartfelt energy of sadness that surrounded the situation.

He said, "This sucks!"

Shelly and Mike began gathering their things to leave and Frankie commented, "Are you guys leaving so soon? I just got here and we haven't talked about the details for the memorial service."

As Shelly continued walking out the door she said, "We're tired, it's been a long couple of days. Just do what you want with the service, I'll talk to you about it later."

By midnight and the memories, the day's events sunk into my brain and I felt like was hit by a brick wall. I felt abandoned and orphaned. Both my parents were gone and I didn't know what to do with myself.

They both had such long lives and their personas were so vibrant. They never let their health or age get in the way of being active or playful. My dad played the congas and harmonica well into his 80's and my mom was out walking every day and lived in the high frequency of joy and love. They were my teachers and my guides. I was now on my own to figure things out.

The next day, reality really set in. We began the tedious process of going through mom's personal items. It was easy for me to see that my mother had issues with my father's death, but buried her pain in buying clothes. It had been a little over a year since I was at the house before my first visit and I was shocked to find my mother had turned the basement into her own personal closet. It was also a surprise that she had clothes in every closet of the house.

My coaching knowledge whispered to me that my mother had a secret. She was a hoarder and was spiritually off-balance. I wondered how long her misery started and felt sad for her loneliness. I looked at the clothes on the racks, many of them still had price tags on them. Most of them brand new and never worn. It didn't make sense to me how a woman so strong in her faith, could be so weak in her addiction to clothes.

♥ Love Beat

It was a negative pattern in her life that never changed. It was fear, the fear of not enough. My mother prayed off every ailment, even the side effects of chemo, but she was still in bondage to "lack" and lived in the energy of "want." I began to find areas in my life that resembled it, I recalled all the times I was in "survivor mode" and lived in the same energy.

I often struggled in two main areas, love and money. It was a constant pattern of lack and when I did have one or the other, I wanted to hold on to it as tight as I could, because I didn't know how long it would last.

In looking at her roomful of impulsive purchases, I came to discover the same energy of fear was a constant in my life that continued to beat me up and knock me down. Fear left me clinging to the ropes, broken and exhausted. I wondered how I could ever get the upper hand and fight off fear.

In my mind's eye I got a picture of a golden wheel inside a wheel, my soul told me they were Chakras and when I read about them I found out they were little spinning energy systems that dwell inside of us to balance our body's energy. I remembered in a few yoga classes where I heard the phrase before but I didn't know much about them. I didn't pay much attention to the prompting, I wasn't in a place of awareness to understand I could use these energy systems to feel better, heal physical ailments and clear out negative energy blocks.

After breakfast my sister came over, and my aunt and I decided to play dress up in mom's huge basement closet. We began to try on hats, shoes and some coats. Shelly opened a coat closet with her hats and pulled out a couple of large hatboxes.

"Look at this one!" she said as she put on a straw cowboy hat. "Look Laurie, this one is for you! It has Toby Keith inside the label!"

"Ha! Ha! Ha! When did mom go country?" I laughed. "Oh Yeah! I like that hat! It has Carolina written all over it! I can wear it to the country concerts!" I put the hat on my head, "Yeeeee-haw!"

Everyone laughed and Shelly put on a hat and it fell over her forehead covering her eyes. "I think that one is too big for you!" I started laughing at how silly she looked.

We kept on pulling out different hats and stacking them on our heads until we had five or six stacked on top. We snapped pictures and kept laughing. We had so much laughter over the humor of the situation that we decided to gather the clothes and give them to a woman's shelter. Knowing the beautiful clothes were going to someone who actually needed them filled us with joy.

Frankie and Bob came back to the house later that morning. Frankie wanted to stop by and ask everyone's thoughts about the memorial service. Bobby came by to be with all of us until he had to go to work. It was a time we needed to stick together and remember our father's wish to take care of each other.

The whole time David was supportive and eager to help with anything we needed. He waited and observed where he could be of assistance. He was there to put my head on his shoulder and he was there to run errands.

A day before her memorial, David went to play golf with Mike and I went to play at a Shaw's Botanical Garden in St. Louis. My sister wanted to take me to a Chinese restaurant that served what she called "Magic Tea." We enjoyed our lunch and being out in the garden. We talked about writing books and she was genuinely happy that David and I were in a relationship.

She said, "You look like you have found yourself. You seem very happy."

"It's odd. I am," I replied. "Even with mom being gone, I still feel her and I know she hung on to meet David." I continued to tell her how she squeezed my hand with approval when I introduced him to her. Her eyes began to water and I could feel her sorrow. I hugged her and we changed the subject.

♥ Love Beat

One of the hardest things for me to do in my life was to talk about my mother in the past tense. She gave so much to me in my spiritual journey of finding forever love. She anchored me with hope, so I would never give up. She prayed for me continually day and night to keep my faith alive. She would never let me quit believing and she always made me forget about time.

I was the big sister who had to stand up for the family, pay my respects and begin the ceremony. The only thing I could say was that my mother was bigger than her body. Her spirit was a giant and everything she did was BIG! I talked about her BIG LOVE and how she loved each of us with a safe pure love. She gave us imagination and playfulness. She made us laugh and dance all the time. Her joy was imprinted in my heart and I had calm delight telling everyone in the room how much she meant to me and how much I would miss her.

The next few minutes became a blur of tears, laughter, condolences and comforting words from caring people who knew my mother. It was a roller coaster of emotional high and lows. I was getting overwhelmed and needed to connect to my sister. I scanned the crowd while the preacher was speaking and couldn't see her.

Somewhere during the appetizers and apologies, she left the service and didn't want to be found. When I realized she had left, I was very disappointed. I was holding in most of my emotions to help my brothers cope. I needed to feel my sister's love energy from the only sister I had.

However, my energy was attracting a similar energy and I felt the hand of my best friend Linda on my shoulder to console me. She hugged me and said, "Oh Laur, I am so sorry. I loved your mom and dad so much!"

"I know you did, Lin. You are family." I held her hand and stood in the back of the room while my mother's pastor stepped up to the podium. Denise and Cindy (my dancing queens) came over to me to give me supportive words and hugs. We were all standing side by side in the hallway and in disbelief. David was helping in the kitchen when he came back through the hallway where we were standing and I began the introductions.

"Why can't I ever get a tall one?" Denise asked jokingly.

"Nice to meet you both!" David said in his hospitable southern style.

I had to go back into the room and David stayed to talk with my friends.

After the service, we packed the car with leftover food, to start a small family caravan back to my mom's home to sort out our lives and figure out how to live without her.

When I arrived, I could see that Shelly left the ceremony early to come back to the house. She had made a couple of cakes and David had made a big pot of spaghetti for us to eat that evening. Shelly was setting the table and getting the house prepared for the gathering. David was making sure he had food for everyone that wanted a plate. He was being that true Southern gentleman.

Later that afternoon, we all gathered around the dining room table where we had so many holiday dinners. While we were eating, my brothers started to bombard David with questions about how we met and how long we've been dating. He was on the hot seat with question after question, but held his own.

He was respectful and funny with his quick one-liners and proved he could compete with my family battle of wits. Frankie said, "I'll go easy on you. It's a good thing for you that I'm grieving!"

We laughed again and served the cakes Shelly made. Frankie took one half of one of the cakes and began to consume it without sharing it with anyone. He washed it down with a tall glass of milk and said, "I'm done! I have to go now."

It was odd to watch him and his wife (who were still separated at the time). He was not only dealing with losing his mom, but also losing his marriage. The rest of us looked at photos and tried on a few more hats and clothes until early evening.

♥ *Love Beat*

Even though we were in pain, it always helped to laugh about the things that were funny to us. We had built a home around love and laughter. We were such a playful family, so we found it inappropriate not to laugh when we were together. Laughter was a form of medicine for me and my family. We could always count on each other to provide a witty phrase or funny comment. Laughter for me was like priming the pump to a joy reservoir.

It was at that point when I noticed my sister Shelly not being very engaging to Frankie. In fact she ignored him much of the time since mom had passed away. It was hard for her to speak with him.

I pulled her aside to find out why she was so silent. She wasn't talking to me either. I figured it was her way of grieving and a house full of people wasn't the best place to discuss it. I could sense betrayal energy all around her, so I didn't want to wait too long before asking her what was wrong. Shelly managed to dodge the question that I asked her about her relationship with Frankie, but I figured time will heal the wounds and dropped the inquisition.

David and I stayed at the house for another week to help get rid of items and to put the house on the market. He hitched a trailer on to his SUV and we brought back a load of things from the house where I grew up.

When we pulled out of the driveway, I looked in the rear view mirror and thought to myself, "I will never be back in this house again." Something tugged at my heart, the long-standing attachment to the home where it all started. It was the house that I remember spinning with unbridled glee to my dad's conga drum. The house where I laughed, loved and found my rhythm.

I looked out the window at the tree-lined streets and heard the sound of children running in the yard. I no longer had a place on Gonzaga Lane. It was now a new era and a new season in my life and my turn to find a new rhythm.

It was the beginning of October and the ride back to Raleigh was breathtaking with the changing of the season. The air was crisp and clean and driving through the mountains was beautifully drenched in different autumn colors. While we were in the mountains of Tennessee, Jenny called.

"Hey, how are you doing?" she asked

"I guess I'm doing OK. You know, mom and all," I replied.

"Laurie, I know this isn't a good time to tell you, but I have to move out of this apartment. You will have to look for somewhere else to live."

I couldn't take one more change; it was all happening so quickly. I asked, "Can't this wait until I get there? We are in Tennessee."

"I know. I'm so sorry, but I have to be out of the apartment over the weekend. Money is tight and I'm moving into a one bedroom," she explained.

Time kept moving in Raleigh without me, but the timing of her request couldn't have been any worse. I told her I would call her when I got to Raleigh. David could see I was upset and asked, "What's wrong? You look like you are sick."

"I am." I really began feeling sick to my stomach and I felt light-headed. I thought it was just because I was so tired or that I just heard I was homeless again.

He asked again, "Please tell me what she said."

"Jenny told me that she has to move out of the apartment by the end of the week to move into a one bedroom."

"Oh, is that all?" he responded very calmly

"Is that all? That's everything! I don't have a home!" I started to cry.

He said, "Well, I was going to ask you eventually and this is sooner than I would have liked, but why don't you just move in with me? You are at my house more than the apartment. We will just take this trailer to my house, empty it and go to the apartment and get your stuff. What do you think?"

I didn't know what to think. I didn't want him to feel obligated to offer me a place to live, but the way he said it was sincere and heartfelt. I told him it sounded like the most logical thing to do. I was really getting too dizzy to think about it. I didn't understand what was going on with my body.

I called Jenny to let her know we were about three hours away and what our plans were going forward. She was overjoyed with our decision to move in together and knew we were meant to be. We arranged to meet in the morning to pick up my things, only the next morning my dizziness got worst. I couldn't lift my head off the pillow.

David called some friends to help him move my bed and other belongings to his house, while I lie in bed holding my head. I had never felt so weird in my life. I couldn't look, move or stand up without holding on to my head, everything was whirling around me.

During the week my symptoms grew worse and David drove me to the doctor. Everything made me nauseous; lights and movement of any kind. I could barely stand the car ride. After the doctor visit, I had been diagnosed with a classic case of vertigo. I was bedridden for two weeks and it took a month for it to clear up completely.

💜 Love Beat

The bout of vertigo was the knockout punch that sent me into myself. I couldn't move and when I did, everything was spinning around. Like the tornado in the springtime, this was a symbol of what was happening to me on the inside.

The loss of my parents was the loss of my foundation and that rocked my world. I felt like I was just a piece of sea grass drifting aimlessly into the abyss. I was not grounded and my body was physically reacting to the spiritual loss. I didn't know that the loss of both my parents would go to the root of my existence, but it did. I had to figure out how I could get my soul back into alignment.

Vertigo caused all my energy to be paralyzed and my head dizzy. All the different emotions swirling around in my head kept me off balance and disoriented. I knew I needed to get help but how and where? I asked my soul while lying in bed and I got my answer.

My soul whispered to me again about spinning energy systems that dwell in our spiritual body called "Chakras." They spin absolute Divine energy into our body at 7 different areas, starting with the root Chakra at the base of your spine. It was during my state of vertigo I could actually see the "fear energy" that was stuck in my root chakra. It was like a wheel with a brake on it. It happened especially when I began to think of myself as an orphan.

When I lost my mother, I could release her from my heart but in it's place was the "Fear of the future." It traveled down and imbedded in my root chakra. It was a negative force I carried the deep in my body.

During my spiritual journey, I was able to pull myself out of the negative thinking pattern into a more heart-centered way of thinking, but I needed to go a layer deeper into my energy system. I learned that I could let in Divine light and love into my chakras to help open and balance them. I could also let negative emotions and energies spin out of my chakras to help me heal. It took almost a month of medication and insights to finally get back on track.

It was now November and I healed from the vertigo and feeling balanced and cleared, I decided to look for work. While at my local coffee shop, I bumped into an acquaintance I met when I first moved to Raleigh. He was the owner of a staffing agency that manned big corporate events and he was looking for someone to help with his business. He hired me on the spot and I was going to work at a full-time job for the first time in almost a year.

Things were finally in balance; I had a great relationship with David, I had gotten through the worst of the vertigo and I was getting along great with David's two daughters. We had invited the girls to dinner and toward the end of dinner after he walked them to their car David got on one knee and proposed.

"What?" I thought that's not how they do it on *The Bachelor*! It is usually a big production number at a fancy restaurant. But right there, in the kitchen, he asked me.

He was totally in the moment and said, "Laurie, you make me so happy. I love you, let's get married. Will you marry me?"

"YES!!!!" I had no doubt, no hesitations; it was green lights all the way!

He told me when he walked his daughters out to the car he told them he was going to ask me, so they should stay out in the driveway until we opened the door.

We both ran out the front door to show them the ring and they were thrilled, but not as thrilled as I was! I stared at the ring over and over. For so long, I had imagined wearing one and hearing the words, "Will you marry me?" I was the happiest person in the world that evening.

I had to start the phone calls to my family. I called Shelly first and let her know that I wanted her to be my matron of honor. She was honored and so happy for me.

I called Frankie to let him know that I was engaged. He had some news as well; he and his wife decided to work things out and they were living together again. My other brother Bob was thrilled to hear the news. Over the phone, we all planned to get together for our first Christmas without our parents.

I called Peg. She was so overjoyed that she wanted to host an engagement party for us with all of our friends.

Getting engaged was like a wellspring of joy coming from my innermost being. I was finally going to be planning my wedding. My head was swimming in details and ideas, color swatches and just joy! I couldn't help my excitement. Some people were a little skeptical and asked me, "Isn't this sort of quick?"

I always responded, "Nope, I've been waiting my whole adult life!"

CHAPTER 11

The Beat of Love

After all the phone calls and congratulations, we got started on finding a wedding date and picked May 27th. It would be Memorial Day weekend (a celebration for the start of summer) and we had already decided to have our wedding at a beach house on Topsail, Island. (The place he grew up going to and the place where we first fell in love.)

It was time to look for a dress and create the theme of my wedding. At first the task was overwhelming but then I morphed into "Producer Laurie" and began to see it as a production.

I thought I would just have fun and research on the Internet for beach wedding ideas and then I took the images and put them in a folder. During the research I began to pick music for different parts of the event: cocktails, dinner, dancing and other chill music during the times we were all hanging out. I began to look for a beach house that would house my dearest friends and could accommodate a beach wedding and reception. I was in heaven planning my big day!

During my pre-planning bliss, my brother called to invite us to celebrate Christmas with them in St. Louis. David and I thought it would be a great idea and planned the trip to be with my family. We all decided it was time for us to make a new memory for the holidays and rented a cabin at Table Rock Lake near Branson, Mo.

I was so excited. Normally I dreaded the holidays, being single. It was the hardest time to maintain my joy. While most people were feeling the warm fuzzies of the holiday season, I had struggled year after year not having a date or a boyfriend. If I had been dating someone during that time, something would always cause us to go our separate ways during the holiday.

For the most part, holidays were just another day of waiting and a stumbling block. I would struggle weeks before the actual holiday and weeks after until I could get my rhythm of life back. It was usually the most difficult time to concentrate on anything else but not having a man in my life.

💜 Love Beat

In my past, the holidays were the worst time for me emotionally. Between the media blitz of Christmas love stories and the family gatherings, I felt out of place as a single woman. It was the hardest time to keep my faith strong and not give up. It was hard not to fall into the energy of "not having" and to keep "wanting."

I tried to stay in joy as much as I could and I would do things that would bring me happiness I would find things to read, dance, and watch movies that made me laugh; anything to not feel sorry for myself. I didn't want to lose my joy, just because I didn't have a boyfriend.

This Christmas would be different. I had a man in my life and I was engaged to him! The only time I was ever this excited for Christmas to arrive was when I was waiting for Santa in my living room as a child.

But that wouldn't be the only thing to make this Christmas different; this was the year without mom and dad around. The choice to celebrate elsewhere was a brilliant idea and I was happy to start new family traditions. I was pleased that David would have the chance to get to know my family better in a different environment.

When we arrived in St. Louis, Linda offered to pick us up at the airport, but we rented a car instead. It was cold and started to snow, but we navigated to her house with no incident.

Linda had a nice warm pot of pasta waiting for us. We ate, talked and got ready to spend the night at her house. We decided to stay overnight and get a jump on the holiday traffic early in the morning.

I looked around her house and couldn't help to notice some of the objects she bought in Ocracoke Island, when we were there. I saw my father's conga drums sitting in the corner.

Linda had made her little bungalow-styled home a beach cottage decorated in beautiful sea colors. It reminded me of the houses in Destin, Florida; decorated in blues, whites, mint green and pale pink. Her rooms had a spa-like feel of a beach oasis with turquoise as the main color theme.

Certain objects reminded me of the time we were on the island and when we bought each piece. I could see it was her safe haven in her sea of emotional storms. It was her safe haven and she was mine.

David, Linda and I stayed up and talked until David got sleepy and bowed out first. Linda and I talked about my wedding for another hour and I heard about her latest love, (or lack of one).

Through the years, we could always count each other for emotional support and a good laugh when it came to the men in our lives. She still struggled with the dark loves of her life. I always tried to see it from a different perspective and give her advice.

♥ *Love Beat*

It made me sad to hear the stories of the men in her life. I knew that she was still trying to crawl out of the" to me "state of awareness (victim mode energy) into a "by me" state of awareness (law of attraction), but it wasn't working fast enough. I tried to tell her there was a place inside of her that needed to be cleared out from all her old energy patterns of love, but there was not enough time to have our usual Dr. Phil moment.

It was now Christmas Eve and we were going to meet my brothers and sister at the cabin, four hours away. The weather reports were saying the weather was bad now, but would be getting worse as the day went on. When we got on the road, it was cold, dark and cloudy. It looked like the clouds were getting so heavy with snow they could pop at any minute! We didn't take much out of the car when we were at Linda's so it was easy to pack up and head out after we ate a small breakfast.

"I'll see you before I leave St. Louis," I said as I hugged her.

"You better!" She said, "Blake will be here and you can see him." Blake was Linda's son, whom I also loved.

"OK, we will for sure! Have a Merry Christmas! I love you, Lin! Thanks for letting us stay!" After seeing her, it was hard to say goodbye. I knew this was going to be a lonely Christmas for her until Blake got there.

"Bye, David!" she yelled from the front door.

I wrapped my scarf around my neck and carefully dodged the ice patches on the driveway to get into the car. We drove away and honked the horn goodbye.

The ride to Branson was interesting, David and I had conversations about my family and the last time we were all together, during my mother's passing, and a wave of sad emotions filled the car.

"I know this is a sad time, but it doesn't have to be," I said. "You know how much I loved my mother, but there is nothing I can do now that she is gone. I have to accept it and use it to help me enjoy the memories about her. She made me laugh and I don't think she would want me to be sad all the time. I don't think she would want any of her children to remember her and be sad. I think she would want any thought of her to put a smile on our face. That's just who she was and that is how I know her the best," I explained. I continued my explanation.

"Honey, that is how I want you to feel about me. When you think of me, I want you to think of me and smile." I said.

"I already do that, Laurie, he said, reassuring me.

I explained, "I mean always! There will be times when you don't want to smile at me, but those aren't the times I want you to think about. I want you to think about me and be happy."

David looked at me puzzled, but he knew what I meant. I think he was puzzled by my philosophy and didn't know if he could accept my psychology about death. He tried to get more answers and we ended up stopping off for lunch to pontificate about the subject.

David always thought more logically and I was the dreamy one and depended more on my intuition in my search for answers. I began to picture us as an image of a guy holding a string to a balloon. I was the balloon out there blowing in the wind and David was holding the string.

David was the one who could hold me in place so I didn't blow away! He grounded me in a way no other man had been able to do. I experienced a feeling of forever love with him. He was my gift and my promise from God. I was happy not to only share my holidays with him, but my whole life. I was ready to marry him right in the restaurant!

♥ Love Beat

My relationship with David was different than any of my other relationships. We had weathered some storms, but that wasn't the focal point of our relationship like so many others. I could see that he was there for me and he made sure he secured my heart with safe and Divine love. By securing my heart and protecting it, I was slowly opening it freely and trusting more. The hurts of the past betrayals were dissolved and I was beginning to celebrate what we were building together. I was open to trust and open to receive the abundance of a loving relationship. The more I celebrated and trusted, the more our love grew and I knew I was becoming more in alignment with my heartbeat and more in rhythm with my future.

The resort where the cabin was located was breathtaking. We traveled the winding snow covered roads up to the lodge. We walked into a rustic log cabin building where the front lobby exhibited the bones of a Great Wooly Mammoth. We went to the front desk and were given a map and the key to the cabin. David and I turned around to walk out the doors to our car, when Santa Claus came in.

He looked like the authentic Santa and he winked at me. "This is going to be magical Christmas!" I gave him a double take; he looked like the real deal to me!

We drove through the winding trails of the property to see it decorated with charming Christmas lights and other holiday decorations. There were lighted animal sculptures throughout the property and I could hardly wait until we could see the displays at night.

The cabins looked like gingerbread houses and wooden cutout chorus members were singing Christmas carols. They had horse drawn carriage tours of the displays.

When we got to our cabin, my sister-in-law Danielle greeted us. She said, "Let's see your ring" and "Let me help you carry something inside!" She grabbed a handful of grocery bags and a suitcase and led us inside laughing. The cabin was warm and cozy with a blazing fire in the fireplace.

"Hey, Sis! You made it! Isn't this place nice?" Frankie came over and gave me a hug. "OK, let's see the ring," he chuckled. As I stuck out my hand, I looked around the cabin.

"Wow! This place is awesome!" I looked around at the vaulted ceiling of the log cabin. It had a beautiful stained glass window where the sun peeped in. The deck had a beautiful view of the lake and the valley below us. The walls were covered in taxidermy throughout the cabin with birds, ducks and antler-handled fixtures on the appliances which were a perfect complement to the decor.

The living room had a Christmas tree tucked in the corner decorated with giant snowflakes and silver and red sparkling ornaments. The kitchen had a large wooden table with a long bench and chairs. The refrigerator was stocked with food for a nice Christmas dinner and my brother made Christmas cookies. We sat in the living room catching up, playing board games and talking about the impending weather.

It was late afternoon when we still hadn't heard from Shelly and Mike about their arrival. We had dinner reservations for that evening at the lodge restaurant and we scheduled a horse carriage ride on the property after dinner. We were starting to get ready for dinner and still hadn't heard from Shelly. I called her.

"Hey, Shell, where are you guys?" I asked. "We are waiting for you to come to dinner."

"We are still in St. Louis. It's too bad to go anywhere tonight," she said. "We are going to stay here with the dogs and drive up tomorrow."

"Are you sure? You can still get here in time. It's not bad here at all." I tried to convince her.

"No, it's really bad now and supposed to get worse. We will be there in the morning. Just tell everyone for me." I could barely get in another word out when she was telling me goodbye and hanging up rather abruptly. I went back into the living room and gave them the bad news.

"Well, that isn't going to stop us from having a good time, is it?" Bobby was annoyed. He didn't seem to want to have to deal with her. I saw his mood change and remembered that Shelly and Bob had a fight before mom passed away.

"No!" We had resolve in our voices and went to the lodge for dinner.

The dining area was decorated in the most interesting mix of old holiday tradition with a twist of rustic ambience in a cozy clubhouse.

The dining area had a corner platform with a piano player playing tunes from Billy Joel and Elton John. We couldn't help making fun of the performer's bad toupee and the old school entertainment for a good few minutes; each joke building from the next.

Still giggling, we sat at the table and tried to stop laughing long enough to look at the menu. We just settled down when my nephew and his girlfriend came walking in.

He looked at our table and said, "I told Marisa that we just had to walk towards the loudest table and that would be ours! I was right!" He laughed again and said, "Merry Christmas! We almost didn't make it. The snow was really coming down hard towards the end of our trip. We kept sliding everywhere we turned!"

"I'm glad you made it safe!" I said relieved. "Sit!" I pointed to the empty place settings. "Here are two spots. We were weren't expecting you until tomorrow, but Shelly and Mike aren't going to make it tonight."

Robbie and Marisa sat down at the table and we offered them the basket of bread. The waiter came quickly over to the table and we ordered something to drink and continued our Christmas Eve dinner celebration without my sister and her husband.

Meanwhile, David was getting closer to my brothers and I was getting to know my sister-in-law. We had time to connect in a great way as she confided in me. She told me that her marriage was restored and that they were ready for a family. I was thrilled and I knew this was a secret prayer answered for my mother.

♥ Love Beat

Learning about my brother's marriage being restored, filled my heart with happiness. I could see the power of forgiveness in action and the power of choice. Choice is the energy of manifestation and I observed it first hand when I made the choice to trust.

After my mother's death and soul searching, my brother was able to find himself and the most important things in his life which were family. We all came together at the cabin with the intention of healing the family and all of our sorrows were turned into joyful memories.

The choice to move forward during difficult times is one of the quickest ways out and the most energetically powerful. Even though it is a challenging task physically and emotionally, energetically it will keep you in alignment of what you are seeking as a final outcome.

I was glad to see they could pull themselves out of the pit by moving forward with their marriage. If my brother and sister-in-law stayed in the pattern of distrust and betrayal then one of them (or both of them) would have been in a downward spiral energetically and their physical world would have fallen apart.

By choice, they decided to stay to work it out and the choice was made from a love driven energy not based on fear-based energy. The decision was made from pure love and their marriage was restored by Divine love.

The cabin provided a new perspective for me about my holidays without my parents. I was creating new traditions, memories and family. I chose to build on the new in my life, instead of what was left in the past. Life had become an adventure for me and my holidays were exciting and pristine.

The cabin gave a family atmosphere in a totally different place. It was something we could all share together and remember forever. After dinner, we walked out into the cold air where there was a horse drawn carriage decorated with lights and a beautiful draft horse decorated with red felt antlers.

We hopped aboard the carriage and there were blankets and hot cocoa ready to keep us warm. We huddled together with the cool breeze in our face. I looked up to see the snowflakes falling with the illumination of the lights, it looked like crystal glass was falling from the sky. It was magical.

I looked at David and snuggled up to him. He had a big smile and looked at me and said, "I love you, baby." It made me warm inside. I knew that I would be hearing that the rest of my life and instantly had an attitude of gratitude. The night was spectacular with the lighted village and the cast of characters that roamed the grounds. It was dressed as Christmas town and seemed like the real deal to me!

After the horse carriage tour, we went back to the cabin to watch movies and to open a few presents. We had an agreement to open one present since Robbie and his girlfriend plans changed and were leaving after breakfast.

The evening went by quickly we were having a great time and decided to play the "Naughty Santa" game since most of us were there. We were going to leave a few presents to play it again when Shelly came the next day.

We successfully brought our holiday spirit tradition to the cabin and we were going to make the most of it. All of us had a great time and made plans to get up early the next morning to make breakfast and open presents when Shelly and Mike arrived.

The cabin was warm and Bobby slept on the couch in the living room. David and I were in one bedroom and Danielle and Frank were in the other, while Robbie and his girlfriend were booked at the hotel just up the hill. We were all safe and snuggled as the snow came down.

The next day the sun came out. It was still cold outside, but knew it was going to warm up to 50 degrees later that day. That was one of the things I remembered about the

Midwest weather; If you didn't like it, wait an hour and it would change.

I could smell coffee coming from the kitchen. Bobby had gotten into a cookie tin. "Mmmmm, these are so freakin' good!" he said with a handful of chocolate chip cookies. He showed me where they were. "Here, have one. I'm making coffee, do ya want some?"

I took a cookie and savored it. "Yeah a big glass of milk would hit the spot with this, but I will have coffee. Where's David?" I asked

"He went to get wood for the fireplace. He said they didn't deliver it last night."

"I'm gonna start making breakfast," Bobby said.

"I think we should wait until more people wake up and get moving around. Then we will call Shell to see when she is coming down," I replied.

"Yeah, I guess that's a good idea." Bobby walked out of the kitchen with a cup of coffee in one hand and the rest of his cookies in the other and sat on the couch. I sat at the table eating my cookie and leafed through a magazine. My cell phone rang and I went back into the bedroom to answer it.

"Hey Shell, are you on the way?"

"No, I'm not feeling well and we haven't left yet. We are bringing the dogs, so we will check them in and then meet you at the cabin. We should get there somewhere around 2 p.m., OK?" She wasn't even apologetic. I didn't understand the reason for all the excuses.

♥ Love Beat

I really couldn't understand her behavior and I got to the point where I didn't care. I didn't want her negative energy to pollute our joy. Everyone at the cabin was making the best out of a tough situation and she was miserable and making it worse.

It was a clear case of "misery loves company." I thought if we could all just communicate with each other and move on, we could get past the pain. Her pain in the situation only amplified more pain; she was actually attracting it the more emotions she fed it. We had found some joy in the situation and chose to build on that. Shelly didn't have a clue as to the healing power of safe love the family had waiting for her.

I walked into my room puzzled and sat on the bed. My brother Frankie noticed I was a little sad and asked if I was ok. I had a tear worked up in my eye and rebuffed the urge to cry. I made the decision to be happy during this time of celebration and I said, "Frankie, will you walk me down the aisle for my wedding?"

"I would be honored," he responded. "Let's mark it on the calendar when you decide on the date."

"We do have a date, May 27th. I will make sure you know so you don't book the band that weekend."

"Ok, sis. We will make it happen."

We both walked back into the living room and David was sitting at the kitchen table talking with Danielle. Bobby was getting the sheets off the sofa in the living room and started packing his things. I notice him and asked, "Where are you going?"

"I think I'm leaving with Robbie and Marisa."

"Why?" I asked puzzled.

"I don't belong here. Everyone is coupled up." He began to tear up and I took him by the hand into my bedroom.

"Bobby, I miss Sue and I know you do too, especially during the holidays. But I have to say, how many holiday gatherings did you see me come alone? Everyone I can think of, that makes about 40 years' worth! I was always by myself at every holiday and you want to leave this once? Bobby, I can't feel sorry for you. It would give me great pleasure if you took the time to know David better. He is your new brother and I want you guys to have a new experience together."

Bob looked at me and said, "You are right, sis. I need to get to know your future husband. That's the right thing for me to do."

I hugged him and said, "Listen, when the time is right you will meet someone. I promise."

💜 Love Beat

I really did have compassion for Bob. He had lost his wife and his mother, but I didn't want him to give up so easily. I knew if he left, he would only drown his sorrows and I felt he needed to be around the love of family. To me it was important for him to surround himself in the safe love energy we could provide for him. It was the support he needed to pull himself through the rough emotional patch. I had to be the voice of reason and speak to his overwhelming emotions for his soul to quiet down and receive it. It was at that moment when Bobby was enlightened to keep himself grounded with the family. We needed each other and energetically it became a safe haven for all of us.

I felt like my mother's spirit was coaching me on what to say and how to reach him. I think it was a defining moment in our relationship and may have saved his emotional life, because six months later he did meet someone.

While making and eating breakfast, we tried to figure out Shelly's weird behavior towards the family. Everyone had a different theory but we didn't let that stop us from enjoying our time together.

Danielle and Frankie decided to walk around the grounds as the sun warmed the trails around the lake. Robbie and

Marissa had left for her family's events. Bobby, David and I hung out at the cabin and played Wii. We were all having fun and I bowed out to wander up the path to the convention center to see what it was like.

The resort was so beautiful that even with naked trees and brown grass, it had a country charm and a homey feel. I roamed the area with gratitude in my heart. I was happy that I could share this time with my family. I walked and said a small prayer to my parents and thanked them for giving me life. I walked back to the cabin and saw David walking towards me on the same path. "I was heading up to the gift shop, and do you want to join me?"

"Sure!" I took his arm and walked with him up the trail.

"This place reminds me of Chetola," he remarked. (Chetola was the place in the mountains of North Carolina where we visited that summer.)

"Yes, it has the same sort of feel to it," I replied.

David and I continued walking around the property. We walked on paths and got to the gift shop and spa. It was decorated in beautiful lights, but was closed for the holiday. It was connected to the lodge and we noticed a leather sofa across from the fireplace with Christmas music playing. We sat down and watched people come in and out of the doorway.

We just enjoyed the moment and sat for a good hour until we felt the need to head back to the cabin.

Back at the cabin was a rousing game of Wii bowling. Frankie, Bobby and Danielle were playing and when we walked in we could hear the roar of a missed pin. We were laughing so hard that I almost peed my pants. David and I joined in the fun while Danielle grabbed a bottle of wine.

"Red or white?" she asked.

"Red!" most of us yelled from the end of the room. She poured a glass for each of us and we continued playing. I looked at my cell phone and I saw I missed a call from Shelly. It was at 4 p.m. and she had called during my walk with David. I called her back and she seemed upset.

"What's up?" I asked.

"We are lost! I don't know where we are we have been driving around for an hour!" She was practically yelling at me over the phone.

"I'll get Frankie. He can tell you how to get here." I handed him the phone and said, "It's Shelly, she's lost."

He took the phone and walked away from the game to navigate her to the cabin. When he came back he told us that she sounded terrible and that she was tired.

We knew that she wasn't in the same frame of mind as we were enjoying our holiday. Her day wasn't as carefree as ours was, but we continued playing Wii. This time it was boxing and Bobby and David were the contestants. We were all yelling and laughing when Shelly and Mike walked through the front door.

"Oh, you finally made it," Frankie sarcastically said. It was now 5 p.m. on Christmas day and we had waited until after 3 p.m. to open our presents. We waited all day to eat any of the cookies or celebrate in our traditional way.

Mike spoke up first, "We got lost coming here and she really doesn't feel well."

"Shelly, I have to show you something. Look!" I put my hand out to show off my engagement ring.

"Wow, that's beautiful!" she said and then she coughed. "I'm sorry, Laurie. I just feel terrible. I am going to go back to the hotel room and take a nap so we can be here for dinner."

"But Shell, I want to ask you to be in my wedding. Will you be my matron of honor?" I asked

"Yes of course, whatever you need. I just have to lie down now." She walked back into the kitchen took a look at the guys (including her husband), playing in front of the television swinging the Wii remotes around.

"I'll see you guys for dinner. Let's go Mike," she barked.

Mike looked at us and shrugged his shoulders. He couldn't believe she wanted to leave 10 minutes after getting there. It puzzled all of us, but we kept on enjoying our Christmas and each other.

We were making dinner that evening and Shelly was late for that event too. She arrived after we waited for her for hours just to have Christmas with her. Our attitude changed. We had already opened presents, played Nasty Santa and ate most of our Christmas cookies and had a great time with each other. We chose to have Merry Christmas without her.

Leaving St. Louis had me perplexed. I had a wonderful time connecting to my brothers in a magical way, but there was a mystery with my sister. David and I spent the day with Linda before flying back to Raleigh.

I asked Linda to be the photographer at my wedding. I knew she would be taking pictures anyway, so I wanted to use her creativity and enjoyment of the beach to capture my event. She was so excited to be a part of my life-changing moment.

Over the next few days, David and I planned a nice quiet New Year's Eve celebration around the neighborhood. We were invited to several parties and didn't commit to any of them, but stopped by them all. The socializing gave me a chance to show off my ring to those who hadn't seen it yet. I couldn't wait to declare the new upcoming year and at the stroke of midnight I kissed David and said, "This is the year for the 'Power of Us!' "

The New Year started better than any year I could remember; I was finally planning my wedding! Everything I thought, dreamed or prayed about was about to come true.

My feelings of excitement were like a keg of dynamite each and every day.

I was thankful for my love for David and anticipating a great life with him. We loved each other with acceptance, affection, appreciation, attention, and enjoyed working together towards our happily ever after.

In a sea of wedding details I played producer, just like I had done most of my life. I had fun with it as much as I could. I made a day of picking the music and visualizing my guests at the reception. I made the decorations that would be aesthetically pleasing. I scouted out the house to lay out the event and looked at where I could place all my décor.

♥ *Love Beat*

I was in a sound state of awareness during the planning of my wedding. It was all that I dreamed it would be. I wasn't just creating an event, but I was creating a lifetime by staying in alignment with the forever love vibration. My creativity was flowing as much as the love energy I was receiving from my friends and David. It was the beginning of my life with love and joy merging at its fullest.

Everything was running as planned, three months before the wedding on my 56th birthday, my brother Frankie called to wish me a Happy Birthday and to give me a big birthday surprise. "Happy Birthday, Sis. Guess what? Danielle and I are going to have a baby!" he excitedly announced.

"Oh my God! That is wonderful news!! I am so excited for you! You have wanted and prayed for a child for a while and now it is happening. How far along is she?"

"Danielle is a couple of months along and we figured it must have happened during our Christmas holiday." He had calculated and discovered the holiday that brought us so much joy and Shelly so much pain.

"Have you told Shelly yet?" I asked.

He sounded disappointed, "I've tried but she blew me off. She hasn't returned any of my calls or invitations. I really don't know what's up with her. Have you heard anything from her?"

"Not really. I called her to talk to her about her bridesmaid dress but that was all. I should be hearing from her this week, when she goes to the store to try it on. I will see if I can find out anything."

I assured him I would speak to her and we shifted our conversation to more pleasant topics, like the baby and the upcoming wedding. I gave him more details about the ceremony, so he could arrange his schedule.

After our conversation, I kept mulling over my sister's attitude towards my family, especially my brother. I couldn't understand why she was so determined to distance herself from us.

About an hour after my phone conversation with my brother, she called to wish me a Happy Birthday as well and to let me know she had tried on her dress and ordered it for the wedding.

I was excited to talk strictly about the wedding, but my curiosity caught up with me. I asked, "Hey Shell, why haven't you talked to Frankie?"

She simply said, "He betrayed my trust. He doesn't respect me."

"Can't you work it out with him? Have you heard the good news?" I was tempted to tell her about the baby.

"What news? Is it about Frankie?"

"Yes, but he should be the one to tell you, not me."

"I don't want to talk to him," she said abruptly.

"Well, I hope you guys aren't still fighting by the time I get married! I don't want drama on my wedding day!" I exclaimed.

"There will be no drama. I wouldn't ruin your special day." She assured me, but when I gave her more details about the housing arrangements she said, "I am not staying in the same house with my brothers!"

I was getting disturbed. "Don't you think you can put your differences aside for one day? Is this about Christmas?"

"Not really." She sounded defensive.

I continued, "We have let all of that stuff go and moved on from it. We are enjoying our lives! I'm about to get married!"

She said, "Laurie, this is more than just a silly fight about Christmas. This is about respect. I have never gotten any respect from him and he betrayed my trust. Maybe it would be better not to have me in your wedding."

"What do you mean? Ask someone else to be in the wedding? Are you backing out now?" I had my limit of her attitude and wanted to make her understand my frustration with her behavior. "You listen to me. I have no mother to help me get ready and no father to walk me down the aisle. I want the rest of family to be with me on my wedding day! I don't care what you have to do, you need to be there for me. I need you with me, Shell."

She said, "That's not what I am saying. I'm not backing out. I just want you to know that it would be too awkward for me to stay in the house. That's how I feel."

By this time, I knew she was set in her decision, but I was not going to have her sabotage my happiness and my joy of the big day. I reassured her that my attempt to have her stay at the house had nothing to do with ambushing her to reconcile with my brothers. In the end, I just wanted to keep my peace and offered to pay for a hotel nearby.

🖤 *Love Beat*

It was my sister's choice to stay in the energy of pain and to resent the actions of the family. I knew this would cripple her, but she made the choice. It was her choice to see it from a victim's point of view. As many times as I thought about the situation I didn't want to feed into her negative victim energy or to "take sides." I made the conscience choice not to get involved with her mind games.

Even though I loved my family, it was important for me not to get engaged in the family chaos. The negative energy would have created discord in my own energy field and I would have been misaligned with my forever love path. I needed to keep the peaceful vibration to prevent any blocks and to keep me grounded. Being grounded in forever love anchored me through the discomfort of my sister's situation and I was able to focus on my wedding day with a clear head.

I rejoiced over the new tools I had to overcome my emotions and was able to look at the situation clearly, embrace it, (by seeing with inner wisdom) and to let it go immediately. There were no struggles, only joy on the other side of it.

I spoke to David about my birthday conversations and he couldn't understand my sister's attitude, but he was comforting and supportive. His motives from that point were to make sure we had the most perfect wedding day as possible without any drama and a drama-free week for everyone at the beach house. I could appreciate his chivalrous actions and continued joyfully preparing for my wedding day.

"What do you think about a low country boil for the reception dinner?" I asked David.

"That's a great idea, especially for the beach house," he replied.

I had an image in my mind about what kind of beach wedding I wanted. I envisioned it a casual, fun experience. I really wanted each of my guests to "feel the love." Which meant, I desired them to immerse themselves fully in the joy experience of being at the beach, to feel the energy of forever love during the ceremony and wholeheartedly celebrate with me in joy.

David and I made our first visit to the rental house on a sunny day in March. We were able to started planning the layout of the tables and met with the caterer and pastor. I was not just imagining my wedding day anymore (as I did my whole life). I was living and breathing it; each day was a day of creation, excitement and execution.

♥ Love Beat

Creating the wedding of my dreams made me realize everything I experienced was created by me. When I chose to make the radical changes within myself, I was able to create something wonderful in my life. I was using my creative power to form my future and I knew if I could create something wonderful, I had the power to un-create by letting go.

I spent next day at the bridal shops with my soon-to-be stepdaughters (who were in their teens) and my flower girl, Lilly (who was seven years old). Each one of them tried on their dress and looked in the mirror. My two stepdaughters looked intently in the mirror at themselves. They remarked about how they looked and how the dress made them feel very pretty.

Lilly's reaction was different; she stepped out of the dressing room, looked in the mirror at herself and with a big smile on her face...she twirled! It was spontaneous and her expression was full of glee! She was so happy to see how pretty she looked in the dress that she twirled!

I remembered that joy of a little girl and I joined her and twirled in front of the mirror. She giggled and I laughed. I laughed to see the sparkle in her eyes each time she saw herself in the mirror and the expression of joy on her face as she twirled. At that moment I flashed back to dancing to my father's conga drum with the same uninhibited expression of joy.

💜 *Love Beat*

I reclaimed my untamed joy the day I let my father go in the conga ritual I had with Linda on our trip to the Outer Banks. Ever since that day, I was living in the state of joy. I remembered glimpses of such a state when I was happily working in my career or during the "God Years."

Joy, for me, was a state of total surrender to the process of remembering myself and loving who I am. I learned it is our natural state of being. Joy isn't just a knee-slapping experience, but it an inner calm delight. I was now residing in the calm delight of a promise being fulfilled. I kept myself in that state of bliss before, during and after the wedding.

Three days before the wedding, David and I took our trip to the beach. We wanted some alone time before the groups of guests arrived. We had family members from all over the world coming in for our wedding.

David was very excited to see his brother from New Zealand and I was anxious to meet him and his wife. I opened my heart with a new perspective, I realized that I was getting a whole new family, instead of dealing with the remnants of my own. It blessed my soul to know I had an extended family, and I no longer had to lead the loner life I had lived for so long. I stopped trying to figure out my sister's disappointing actions, released her and began to focus on each and every moment of my joy filled life.

♥ *Love Beat*

I made the conscious effort to fully be present in my wedding weekend bliss. I learned throughout my life that some things in life would never be answered, but I should just learn to trust things will work out. My sister and her reasons, any problems with wedding and any other trivial issues would not get my attention, I didn't focus on anything that would steal my joy.

I learned to detach myself of any entanglements that brought negative energy to me by releasing it as soon as I recognized it. I had to release all expectations and all attachment to them. I had to be neutral like a blank page to let the story unfold, with no judgment or emotion. I let Divine love carry me through the day and as I did I felt the forever love energy build inside of me and around me like a shield.

When David and I checked into the rental house, we started having fun. I made signs for the doors of each couple's room and I spent the afternoon at the pool with my sister and Jenny who came earlier than the other guests. David was back at the house helping my guests get situated in the house and I arrived later to visit with them all.

It was a glorious day! The sun was shining, the breeze gently blowing cool air off the rolling surf. The ocean was rhythmic and hypnotic. We found beach chairs and gathered them on the beach, I made a pitcher of margaritas and we sipped them as we caught up. Everyone was having such a light-hearted good time. I was in heaven!

On May 27, 2012, my wedding day finally arrived! I got up early, put on my robe with "Bride" written on the back in blue rhinestones and poured a cup of coffee. I could see my flower girl standing by the fence of the balcony watching the waves of the ocean. I slid open the screen door and joined her.

"This is the big day! Aren't you excited?" she asked and giggled.

I kneeled to her level and gave her a hug. "I have been waiting for this day my whole life! Yes, I'm really excited!"

We stood together watching the waves roll in while the sun came up over the horizon. It was a spectacular brilliant orange and the sky was a "Carolina" blue. The seagulls were flying and among the sound of crashing waves I could also hear people stirring in the house waking up.

David had stayed the night with his brother John from New Zealand who had rented a beach house a few houses from ours and I could see him walking the beach towards us. He waved and came up the boardwalk of our house.

"Hi, Honey! Happy wedding day!" I cheerful greeted him at the foot of the stairs. "Did you sleep OK?" I asked.

"Yeah, I did. How about you?" he responded.

"Yes, I was talking with Dyann and Rose (my Atlanta Ya Ya sisters) until about midnight and then we all went to bed. Did you have breakfast?"

"No, that is why I came over, to make breakfast and to visit before the party supply people come over to drop off the tables and chairs," he said.

David had a cup of coffee. I had platters of fruit and croissants opened and he made eggs and bacon. We cracked a bottle of Prosecco and made mimosas for anyone who wanted to get started early with the celebration.

My bridal party and I had a reservations to get pedicures and manicures while the rest of the guests were going to lay out at the beach until the delivery of the party supplies to decorate the house for the wedding reception and the arch for the ceremony.

I was determined not to get into the producer role on this day, even if it killed me! I had to fight off feelings of worry and having to control the event but I finally just surrendered to being a bride and kept myself relaxed.

♥ Love Beat

It was a difficult task to switch my brain off and just enjoy the moment. I was always jumping back and forth from the producer role to the bride role until I felt the energy of peace reside in my heart. I thought whatever happens will happen and if I spent the time thinking of little details, I would miss my wedding. I knew love and worry didn't mix and chose to turn off worry and focus on enjoying the moment of love, to let go and go with its flow.

This was an important lesson for me as a "Type A" personality, but when I learned to lean into my fear of "it not being perfect"- the perfectionism began to fade away and so did the worry and anxiety. Love was bigger than fear.

I came back to the beach house to find everything in place and the arrival of my friend Linda and her son Blake. It was so good to see her and she was thrilled to be there.

She had also brought my dad's conga and we were going to dress it with a teal colored Zumba skirt and it was going to be down by the arch during the ceremony. I had white roses for each of our parents that we lost and put them on top of the conga drum. It was a beautiful scene and the emotion of it all put a lump in my throat.

I thought of all the times my mom would pray for this day and how she coached me through the loneliest times of my life. She would always tell me to believe and thank God for making it happen even though it hadn't. I could hear her say, "Laurie, God is working behind the scenes to make your dreams come true."

I would always feel comforted and my trust in God would come alive. The joy of my heart's desire would rise up and I would know that my loneliness was a temporary condition.

♥ *Love Beat*

I learned in my spiritual journey through the different loves energies I encountered in my life and my faith, forever love is what I was in search of and wouldn't settle for any other love. I gave myself the gift of inward healing and listened to my higher wisdom to let go my negative patterns. I embraced change when it happened and I learned to listen to the rhythm of my heart. It changed the way I saw myself and slowly began to love myself in a healthy way. David's safe love gave me courage to trust again and in my wholeness, I opened my heart to receive his love.

As I got ready to walk down the aisle, I saw Lilly. She said, "Laurie, look at me!" and she twirled.

I took her by the hand and twirled her. We both giggled and then I said, "Look at me!" I twirled. When I did, the joy of the Lord came upon me and I began to laugh. I could feel the forever love energy envelope me and keep me.

It was time. We all got in position on the boardwalk and I could see my friends and family gathered on the beach waiting for me to come down the aisle.

My brother Frankie took me by the arm and we began the walk down the boardwalk and onto the sand. I could remember only dreaming about such an event, but I was living my dream. I felt blessings all around me and it seemed as if God was smiling down at our union.

Our preacher was the most incredible usher of the presence of love and joy. He performed a meaningful ceremony with symbolism about the sea and the beach. People that were in the audience where deeply touched and moved from the energy that surrounded our ceremony. They could feel the tangible presence of forever love.

In front of my best friends Linda, Peggy and Jenny, my YaYa sisters, family and the Universe I stood at the altar of the sea and sky. I looked at my husband to be and beyond David's loving blue eyes, in an instant, I saw a flash of my future with him laughing, smiling and enjoying the rest of our lives.

"My promise of forever love is fulfilled," I thought to myself as I held his hand.

In one breath I said, "I do." I said yes to forever love.

♥ *Love Beat*

Our vows to each other are what is called "tying the knot." Energetically, we created a bond and a claimed our own imprint that said, "I am yours and you are mine." We literally tied ourselves together energetically with the intention of forever love. We were perfect reflections of each other and we mirrored each other's desires. We both had heart-conscious desires and were energetically matched. In our marriage vows we created a forever love bubble and tied a knot from our wholeness. We were perfectly aligned with the Universe and our destinies.

Almost one month after we said our vows we moved to one of the most exciting and beautiful places in the United States, Key West. It is bursting with high energies of joy and peace. Tourists flock to our island to escape the realities of life, while I enjoy living my dream. I am grateful that I can share this journey with my husband David, whom I waited for my entire life and now the best is yet to come.

EPILOGUE

The Beat of Bliss

Just before I finished writing this book, my husband and I decided to take a little boat trip out to the coral reef. I was very excited to go since it was usually too windy for us to get out there in our 17- foot boat. But the weather and waters were perfect for this trip.

I was preparing myself to take another spiritual journey, to go deeper into the manifestation of the next phase of my life. I would like to share the experience with you as a guide to what a spiritual journey can be look like when you open your mind and heart to embrace it.

Our day started out with bright sunshine and calm winds. The waters were as blue as the sky with the waves gently rocking the boat. We observed the weather as we slowly departed from our slip and putted out of the marina. It was a wonderfully perfect day to set a new course.

David said, "I'm not going out the way we usually do, OK?" I thought to myself normally we go where there is less wind but it is a longer way out to the ocean. I was convinced David's skill and knowledge would keep me safe to go a different way. I prepared myself for the excitement of a new course.

I set my intention for this experience, I wanted to learn about expansion. I had been secretly praying and believing for expansion for a few weeks but I was actually feeling it when we got in the boat. I was feeling the energy of limitlessness and the expansive energy of the ocean. I was totally enjoying my view.

When we got to the channel markers that were dug deeper to dock the cruise ships the waters were rough and not flowing congruently. It was a made our boat rock and it an uncomfortable ride. The rough waters meant something more. The waves were getting rougher and the boat began to sway. A big wave hit the boat and David adjusted its speed to slow down the boat. While I was holding on to the side to brace myself for another wave, I heard a soul whisper, "It's not always going to be easy. But, if you make the adjustments, you will be able to navigate the rough waters." So it is with life and love that when we are in situations that make us uncomfortable, if we can just slow down and hear our inner wisdom instead of rushing into the situation, we can make the ride more enjoyable.

David navigated through the rough currents with ease and we were flowing along with the gentle waves of the ocean once again. I began to enjoy the ride as I looked out into the waters. My husband pointed a finger out in the direction to the right of our boat. "Look Laurie!" It was a pod of dolphins swimming alongside of us.

"There are my little friends!" I said out loud. I loved the dolphin energy. I had always loved them, but I felt a kinship to them now and I didn't know if it was because I live near the ocean or if it was something else. As soon as I saw them, it filled me with excitement and I flashed back to the dream I had when my mother was ill.

Instantly, my soul understood the dream of the shipwreck. I had sent an intention for expansion and I was ready to receive my first deposit. In my dream, after my mother jumped off the ship to end her physical life, when I saw the air bubbles stop coming to the surface, the dolphin appeared and gave me a smile as it surfaced. The secret that he implied when I looked in its eye was that he dwelled in an abundant state of joy frequency.

The smiling image of the dolphin was a symbol of my mother's spirit and the revelation brought me calm delight. I had a peaceful sensation run through my body like electricity and the root of joy firmly planted deep in my heart.

I had a deep knowing that my mother's spirit would always be with me, especially when I saw a dolphin. I could still think of her beauty, joy and healing touch. I could think back to the times of when the healing energy of the dolphin helped me through the loneliest times when I was a single woman just as my mother did throughout my life. Since I was married, the dolphins brought clarity as their healing energy.

I could see the channel markers as my husband navigated through the deep and shallow waters. Mapping out the course to the reef with the abundance of sea life.

I also viewed the channel markers as symbols of my love life and could vividly see how they plotted the course of my life through the different love energies. Helping me to navigate through the deep and shallow emotions throughout my life and to put me on my course to abundance today.

♥ Love Beat

My journey of love beats mirrored the channel markers. It started with the shallow waters of lower love energies that made imprints of attraction to the opposite sex. I was living in the low energy of "longing" based on a fear of time and my frequency was advertising this type of low energy to the Universe, which attracted the wrong type of men. My energy was actually repelling the very thing that I longed for!

It began when I was young and I allowed the "Time Bomb" game take away my self-love and planted a seed of lack into my soul. It fragmented my heart and from that point on Randy, John, Anchor Boy and Mr. Fabulous were just other channel markers along the way to finding myself and most of all loving myself. Each man helped me realize a part of me that was missing.

Randy was attracted by the "pick me" energy of youth and his dark love intentions reflected the "want" energy that I carried inside of me. When the relationship ended, I carried around a dark love energy, which imprinted me as powerless and a victim.

John was attracted from the "struggle" energy, where I was struggling between what I wanted and who I was. Our relationship was always a struggle and imprinted on my heart that "love was a struggle" and "I didn't trust in love."

From the" want" energy, I attracted Anchor Boy and when he cheated on me, I was imprinted with distrust.

I finally asked for help and God heard my cries. Divine Love shook off all the old negative imprints that had been created in my heart and replaced it with an imprint of joy. He restored my power but not my wholeness.

The years went by, but by the age of 50 I began to be more aware of time. By focusing on time and the fear of it, I attracted Mr. Fabulous. Mr. Fabulous was the strongest attraction of all, because I used the Law of Attraction to get him. However, my attachment to him led to abuse. In my mind, he was my Superman and I was his damsel in distress. He was a reflection of the energy that was inside of me. He was produced by the lower energies of "yearning" and the belief of "this is my last chance" that battled within me.

By the time I reached 55, I was able to release things from my past and let them go. I became aware of my role in creating my life's journey. I learned about the different love energies and was able to clear the old blocks of negative energy. I knew in my heart that God/Source was depositing Divine Love into my being and I was able to receive it.

I recognized when two people come together they are energetic beings coming together and exchanging energy. This energy creates sort of love bubble enclosure that is magnetic and a reflection of all the combined energies we both carry. The energies that we carry within us, reflect back to us and that is how we find ourselves dating the same people over and over. Unless we are healed and whole, cleared from all negative patterns of the past, we will never really know our true selves to become true loves.

I finally realized that all my struggles in love were for my highest good, whether they seemed that way or not. Instead of letting them destroy me, they caused me to find myself and my soul was restored.

We finally reached the reef with it an abundance of sunshine, fish and beautiful views. I looked down at the waters and could see a multitude of brightly marked fish, while my husband was getting his fishing gear ready. I could see the joy in his eyes as he got his tackle box opened and I got prepared to stake my claim on one side of the boat to bask in the glory of the moment.

I stared at the vastness of the ocean and took a deep breath in. I could feel all of my charkas open and spinning, letting love and light in an out of my being as if I was radiating the energy. I resonated with the energy of the water and the waves as I breathed out a large sigh. I felt the gentle rocking of the boat and the peace that was dwelling inside of me.

"Look, honey. There's another dolphin!" I pointed out to the bough of the boat.

"This is a great day to be out here," he said.

"Every day is a great day! I replied joyfully.

I watched the dolphin surface and go back down into the clear blue waters. I was surrounded by the energy of peace, expansiveness and joy. Everything looked like it was going in slow motion as I had my eyes fixed on the location of the dolphin, hoping to see him again.

I took a deep breath in and was mesmerized by reflection of the sun hitting the aqua blue waters. The healing energy from the dolphin spoke to my heart, "You are in a state of bliss.

Remember this feeling. It is how we live. Stay in your joy, stay in your bliss. Love heals the heart but joy transforms it."

I didn't see the dolphin surface again, but I felt as if the he was an angel of the sea, speaking right to my heart sending me to a new state of awareness. There was a tranquil almost euphoric energy that permeated my body. I didn't observe the ocean in the same way and I didn't envision love the same way either.

My life was so different from the road that took me here. I am happily married to a wonderful man whom I adore and living the Florida lifestyle, just as I envisioned it to be.

But I am different, I have changed my frequency to live in a high vibration of joy and love. My spiritual heart journey led me to a place I had never been, it led me to abundance, balance and bliss.

I have a new perception of what love means to me now and want to share it with the world. Being on the ocean that day made lose attachment to all the old beliefs I had about love. The ocean became a new metaphor for love. There are two parts of the ocean. If you look at just the ocean in its natural state; it is deep, full of abundant life and expansion, but the second part are the waves.

♥ Love Beat

Love is like the ocean in its natural state; it is a neutral a field of emptiness and it is the source of life. It is limitless and has no boundaries. It has no highs or lows only the deeper waters and vastness. The waves, on the other hand, are the ocean's ecstatic state. The tides rise and fall, the currents change with the wind. Waves can be erratic or calm. They can wreak havoc or they can be tranquil. The ocean can exist without the waves, but the waves cannot exist without the ocean.

In love, there are waves of excitement, arousal, feelings of ecstasy and the source of emotions within. Emotions are like the waves that make us feel sensations of love. But when that all the ups and down of emotions disappear what is left?

Energy.

The real spiritual journey is returning to a place of emptiness to let God/Source ground and root you by all your experiences for your greatest good and to come the place of self-love.

Forever Love is settling into a place of neutrality or a deep peaceful state of being. It is not striving to chase it, search for it or manipulate it into what you want, but letting the Divine guide you to the same vibration of loving yourself and clearing old energy blockages.

You will begin to hear the heart rhythm of your true self and will be able to align with the energy that will magnetize you to your forever love mate. When your vibration matches your true self, your true love will be drawn to you and the synchronicity of the Universe will work in harmony. You will attract the things you want from the wholeness of your true self and not out of the energy of "want" or "struggle."

I looked up at David catching one fish after another. I saw the joy he had in the moment and was grateful of experience together. "We are perfect together," I thought to myself.

In the middle of the ocean, I realized that I attracted David when I was in my wholeness. I wasn't completely whole, but I was in a higher state of awareness and God/Source met me where I was.

I finally got it!

💜 *Love Beat*

I learned to release the unsavory moments of my past to bring me to a place of balance. When I was able to unite at every level of myself (body, soul and spirit) I began to receive the creative energy of choice. It is the energy that opens us up at every single level and it's the energy that helps us to see how we have been choosing. Choice opened me up to see that through my actions, I magnified creation. All energy I gathered through my focus, through my belief systems and through my thoughts were all I created by me. I learned to let ALL energy support me. I released my fear of time and I discovered a new energy to allow me to make choices that would empowered me at every level to feel the light of Source, the light of who I AM and the light of love.

I am perfectly Pisces and perfectly happy. I'm both of the fish swimming in different directions, (the yin and yang). I am flowing in the feminine and flowing in the masculine energy in balance and kept in perfect harmony with my new heart beat rhythm. I swim in my awareness of all that I am. I learned that when you're seeking forever love you are in perfect timing because time no longer exists. Your heart becomes open to timelessness, limitless abundance and endless joy. I dwell in an expansive state of forever love by loving myself and loving my man. I stay plugged into the abundance of joy and I am loving life.